The Season of Singing Has Come

A Muslim woman, an encounter with Jesus, a life changed

Shaadia Firoz
Translated by Phil Shenk

D0347813

Authentic

First published 2018 by Authentic Media Limited,
PO Box 6326, Bletchley, Milton Keynes, MK1 9GG.
authenticmedia.co.uk

British Library Cataloguing in Publication Data
A catalogue record for this book is available from the British Library.
ISBN: 978-1-78078-466-3
978-1-78078-467-0 (e-book)

Cover design by Vivian Hansen
Printed in the UK by CPI Group (UK) Ltd., Croydon, CR0 4YY

'The agenda has changed – now people of Muslim heritage are not only changing faith-allegiance to Christ but publishing their story. *The Season of Singing Has Come* is one such story – balanced and compelling, it is a journey that ended at the realization that religious rituals are simply "unnecessary" and that relationship with the living God by faith in Jesus, is essential.'

Steve Bell, speaker, author and National Director
for Interserve (Great Britain & Ireland)

'Shaadia's story takes the reader through a roller-coaster of images and emotions, thoughts and prayers as one follows the narrative of her life. It is a biography of redemption that does not ignore the darkness, abuse and brokenness that are also part of life. As the author writes, "The past is part of your life, and you can't ignore it, or pretend to forget it." As one reads her stories, there is the deep sense that God's Spirit is always present, even when such presence isn't known to those involved in the various conflicts and tragedies. It is this gift of a Spirit-led life that makes the book a wonderful resource for healing and hope, and a reminder that God's love is far greater than we could ever imagine or dream.'

Dr C. Rosalee Velloso Ewell, Principal,
Redcliffe College, Gloucester

'In these days when increasing numbers of Muslims all over the world (including the Caucasus) are turning in faith to Jesus Christ, it is most helpful to read this warmly personal and challenging testimony.'

Martin Goldsmith, author, international speaker
and associate lecturer, All Nations Christian College

Contents

Author's Word

No one lights a lamp and hides it in a clay jar
or puts it under a bed. Instead, they put it on
a stand, so that those who come in can see the
light. For there is nothing hidden that will not
be disclosed, and nothing concealed that will not
be known or brought out into the open.

Luke 8:16,17

The idea of writing this book began to stir in me long ago. At first, the thought seemed far-fetched and completely unrealistic. But over the course of time, I came to the strong conviction that it was the will of God for me to write it. And that if it was his will, I would be able to do it! I write out of a wellspring of deep love and thankfulness for what the great Creator of the universe – my Creator – has done on behalf of this world and personally for me.

This book is written with the fervent desire that it will penetrate the heart of each person who reads it, regardless of their personal or faith background. My sincere prayer for you, my dear reader, is that the Most High God will generously bless you with all of his goodness, especially a true knowledge of his good plan for you and of his truth that sets you free, heals you, and gives you love, peace, joy, hope and eternal life.

What is before you is a frank, sincere life confession, without any cosmetic decoration. I have taken off the mask that I wore for years to hide the shame and sorrow of my life. Certain episodes may appear to you to be overly candid and transparent, but such is the honest reality of life. My life is a testimony to the transforming power of God's love.

Let's make an agreement that while you are reading this book, you will take off your mask and read with an open heart. There are no coincidences with the Eternal God. I do not know who you are. Whoever you may be and whatever background you may have come from – Christian, Muslim, Buddhist, atheist, or any other – this book is for you. Read it to the end.

N.B. Names of people and places have been changed for security reasons.

> *Yet you desired faithfulness even in the womb;*
> *you taught me wisdom in that secret place.*
> *Psalm 51:6*

Part One

Lost

But he was pierced for our transgressions,
*   he was crushed for our iniquities;*
the punishment that brought us peace was on him,
*   and by his wounds we are healed.*
We all, like sheep, have gone astray,
*   each of us has turned to our own way;*
and the LORD has laid on him
*   the iniquity of us all.*

*   Isaiah 53:5,6*

1

Loveless Beginnings

I was born in 1967 in a rural village of one of the Soviet Socialist republics in the North Caucasus region near the Caspian Sea. My family was Muslim, influenced both by residual communism and strong Muslim religious traditions.

I knew nothing about Jesus Christ as Lord and Saviour, and didn't want to know anything about him. I could not imagine then that he would have anything to do with my destiny. As far as I knew, Jesus was a prophet, the Muslim religion was the one true faith, and all those who did not follow Islam were the unfaithful ones who would burn in hell. First and foremost among the ranks of these infidels were the Christians, that is, the Russians, for we assumed there was no difference. Only much later did I discover that Christianity carries no nationality, and Russians have no greater closeness or distance from true Christianity than anyone from any other ethnic background.

Years went by before I understood the reality of how the Islamic religion had been planted in my part of the world by Arab followers of Mohammed. Under their powerful onslaught, many Caucasus peoples submitted centuries ago to Islam and to the intense influence of Arabic culture. I was shocked to discover that some of my ancient ancestors had been believers in Isa Masikh, as Jesus Christ is called in Arabic, and in his death on the cross for the sins of the world. Many were killed for refusing to convert to Islam.

But as I grew up, I was proud to have been born a Muslim, sincerely believing that Islam was the religion of peace and goodness, as I had been told. With all my heart I searched for a close relationship with Allah – just like millions of honourable people in Muslim cultures around the world today. My story, however, is of the lack of peace in my heart.

There was no love in my family, growing up. My father drank heavily. Most of the money he earned went towards his own drinking and hosting his drinking buddies at our house. Due to his spending on alcohol, we were often in financial straits, even though he earned good money. At times there was no food in the house. I almost always had to wear old, worn-out clothes. My mother went into debt to keep the household going. When he was drunk (and he was drunk most of the time), my father was very aggressive and cruel both to my mother and to us children.

We never addressed him as 'father', which enraged him even more. For me, there was simply no way that I could use that term in reference to him. The hateful words 'Get out of my house!' accompanied by other vile language and horrible insults, were often heard in our home. 'Father' was a painful word to me. My soul tightened in fear whenever I heard his voice or heard my mother say that Father was coming. Mama loved us as she was able, but she couldn't protect us from our father; sadly, she herself didn't know what peace and happiness felt like.

I was four or five years old when I felt so sad and distressed because of my father's behaviour that I decided to run away. At that time we lived four kilometres from our home village, in a location where my father was taking care of livestock. Our living quarters were just a tiny hut in which our whole family lived. Seizing a moment when no one saw me, I left the hut and started walking by myself down the road in the direction of the village. With all my heart I did not want to ever return to that situation. Halfway to the village a woman, who seemed good-hearted and kind, met me along the road. She began to gently inquire of me as to who I was and where I was going. Hoping that she would take pity on me and take me with her far away from my father, I responded that I was an orphan and that I was without anyone in the world. She asked me if I would like to become her daughter and go with her to live in a big city. I responded that, yes, I would like that very much.

I was so happy to have met her! But, due to the direction she was going, it was necessary to go back the way I had come – right past that little hut. In my childhood naivety, I thought my family wouldn't notice me, and I would get to live peacefully in the big city with this kind aunt. But my mother, having noticed that I was missing, had gone out on to the road to look for me. So, the short adventure of a little girl seeking a new life came to an abrupt end. I remember the overwhelming disappointment in my little-girl heart that day when my mother, thinking I had merely got lost, sent me back inside our hut.

We were six children in the family – a brother, followed by five sisters. I was the middle girl. When I was a little older, I came to realize that my official last name was from my mother's family line. This was true also of all my sisters. Only my brother bore my father's family name. In the culture in which I grew up, the birth of a daughter is not as honourable as the birth of a son. Sometimes it is even considered shameful. Of course, not everyone in the culture carries this outlook, but more than once in my childhood I heard people say, 'It's better to give birth to a stone than a girl; at least a stone is valuable for building.' All the blame for the birth of a daughter lay on the shoulders of the mother, but when a son was born, the father was treated as a hero.

In our family, when the fifth daughter was born, my mother went into such a heavy depression that she refused to breastfeed the baby and didn't even want to see her daughter. For the first several days another young woman in our village nursed my little sister. This young woman had given birth to a baby about the same time as my mother.

I was seven years old at the time, and I vividly remember a woman from the village coming to my house with the expressed intent of taking my little sister into her family. My mother had experienced a type of temporary emotional breakdown, and I clearly understand now that she wouldn't really have wanted to give her baby away, but in village life gossip spreads quickly. I was truly frightened by the idea that my mother was going to give my sister away. By the time this woman came, my mother had come to her senses. She was not willing to give her little daughter away to anyone. My joy at this knew no bounds because I loved my baby sister so much.

I don't know why my father didn't want to give his daughters his family name. Perhaps he was ashamed of having daughters one after another. Or maybe he had another reason. I'm not certain whether he himself knows the answer to this question; or whether he understands the deep pain which my sisters and I, along with our mother, experienced because of this.

Our living quarters became more and more like a barn. Several times my father threw everything out of the hut and seemed to be attempting to set it on fire with my mother and us children still inside. In those moments he seemed like a maniac, trying to kill us all.

It was very embarrassing for me to bring a friend home, and truly shameful when an adult came to visit. I constantly dreamed about a normal home and a peaceful life. One day an aunt, who always smiled and spoke kindly to my face, didn't know I was listening. 'She is the stupid daughter of that drunken idiot,' she blurted. I went off by myself and cried bitterly. I had believed that she thought highly of me and loved me. In my childish reasoning, I concluded that adults are liars and hypocrites, which meant that this world in which I lived was full of untrustworthy deception.

All of the most devastating memories of my childhood are associated with my father. Out of all my childhood, there is only one vivid exception to this. My father was shepherding a flock of sheep up in the mountains, and one day he spent the afternoon peacefully conversing with three of his daughters while sitting beside a mountain stream. That day he had not been drinking – he was completely sober.

He listened to us, and we shared with him our needs and feelings. So peaceful and kind was he that my heart overflowed with hope and warm feelings towards him. Was I dreaming? All of those bad things seemed no longer to exist. I fully believed that from then on everything would be good. But, alas, the next day life went back to 'normal' as he began to act in the old horrible ways again. It was like a season where for weeks, rain and cold and gloominess prevail, and then one day a bright sun appears only to disappear again just as quickly.

In the months following, the world seemed more hopeless than ever. Nonetheless, that one day stuck far back in a corner of my mind, like a far-off fairy tale.

My sister, Zagidat, was two years older than I. When Zagidat was three years old, our drunken father brutally beat her. Of course, I was too small to remember, but my older sister and my mother told me later. When Mama came home that day, little Zagidat was blue and swollen almost beyond recognition. Her face was distorted with terror and pain. She was in such shock that she couldn't emit so much as a sound, and my father continued to beat her. Zagidat never spoke again. Her mental development was slowed, but she was always kind and fond of small children.

One hot summer when I was ten and Zagidat twelve, we accompanied our parents to the lower meadows where they grazed the livestock of our collective *kolkhoz* farm and a few of our own. Zagidat became frightfully ill. She suffered terribly. It was even worse that she couldn't talk to tell us what she was feeling. Father arrived at his personal diagnosis and announced that she would die if she drank even a tiny bit of water. The terror that all of us felt in the presence of our father was so intense that I feared that she would indeed die if we gave her a drop of water. But Zagidat was obviously suffering from pain and terrible thirst. She moaned and cast her glance towards the jug of water at the doorway. She completely stopped eating and went a number of days without any food.

Several families worked together with livestock that summer in this farm pasture. Fruit of any kind was such a rarity that sometimes in our village I would pick up a dirty scrap of apple right off the ground and happily stuff it in my mouth. That summer my mother told me that on a hillside not far from the *kolkhoz* farm pasture, there were mulberry trees. She suggested I go there with the other children and gather mulberries. Perhaps Zagidat would be able to eat a few of those. I rejoiced at the possibility that I could bring back something tasty for my sister that she would eat and not refuse.

Although Zagidat couldn't talk, it was clear that she understood my plan. Genuine joy shone on her face when she realized that I was going to gather mulberries for her.

Our group of children was led by a girl several years older than I was. She was a powerful girl – the headstrong and egotistical daughter of one of the chiefs of our village. When we reached the mulberries, there weren't as many as we had hoped. This girl forbade the children whom she considered unworthy from taking any and even blocked our approach to the tree. As the daughter of the local drunk, I was first in the 'unworthy' category. All I could think about was Zagidat waiting for me to come back with mulberries. I didn't want to fail her. I pleaded with this girl, explaining and trying to arouse in her some compassion for my sick sister, but she was completely unresponsive. Not only did she refuse me, but she threw stones to force me away. When she smashed the collection jar I had brought, my last hope for my dying sister disappeared.

This powerful girl and her circle were jubilant and merry throughout that whole afternoon. Returning to our place, I felt like the most miserable worthless person on the face of the earth. Streams of tears ran down my face. Zagidat waited with joy, certain that I would return with mulberries for her, but I had failed her. My heart broke from the unbearable pain that I had been so weak, incapable, such an abject failure, in this crucial task.

When she realized that I had returned with nothing, Zagidat looked at me with deep despair, and tears rolled down her cheeks. Three days later she died.

I was an impressionable and sensitive child. This vision of my dying sister, suffering under the brutal commands of my father – along with the knowledge of my failure to help her – tormented me for many years to come.

The image of my father instilled such terror in me that I often wished him dead. I awakened with nightmares of him brutally cutting my little sister into pieces. I longed for him not to exist. As a young girl, I seriously thought about how I could murder him. I remember coming up to my mother with this 'wonderful' plan and an axe in my hands, telling her that I was going to kill our father, to rescue her and my sisters from all the suffering. My brother was the oldest in the family and he had left for further study because in my village the school only had eight grades. How happily we would live then, without my father! I think I was under eight years old. Of course, I was not capable of actually killing him; this desire was only the mute cry of my desperate, childish spirit. Nonetheless, I constantly dreamed of life without him, and envied those friends who had no father.

I hated and feared my father with every fibre of my being. Many nights, even though I was terrified of the dark, I hid in the darkest alleys of our neighbourhood for long hours. While most of my little friends were asleep in their beds, I was out there trying to stay away from my drunken, enraged, out-of-control father. My fear of him was stronger than any other fear. My greatest joy was when my father took a long trip far away. Then I could relax and sleep peacefully – the happiest, freest child on the planet.

My father often brought his drinking buddies home for carousing. One of those nights one of my father's friends, a distant relative, asked my father if he could take me home with him overnight. I must have been seven or eight. I clearly remember how he argued my father into agreeing by saying that there were women at his house, and they would watch over me.

It was extremely late when we arrived at the man's house. Everyone else appeared to be sleeping. He made me lie down beside him in his bed where he began to breathe heavily. He feverishly rubbed against me and ran his hands over my body. Even though I was only a child, and didn't grasp most of what was going on, I fully understood that something was horribly 'not right' about this revolting situation. He didn't actually rape me, but what he did was enough to scar me with a devastating feeling of degradation and uncleanness.

Finally the man fell asleep. I lay there for hours in the dark room unable to close my eyes, paralysed with fear and horror. Through the open window the night sky and the bright moon were visible, as if trying to comfort a terrified little girl.

Suddenly in the middle of that night came a piercing shriek, full of pain and fear. It was the shriek of our schoolteacher being brutalized by her drunken husband. Their house was not far from where I lay. But no help came. In that culture, the man is the master of his house, and there is no authority to check him.

When I could get up the following morning, I was happy to see that there were women in this house where I had been forced to spend the night. But these women related to me with icy silence and hostility. Maybe you can feel with me the bitter disappointment that consumed me. Typically, as a child, I concluded that I was somehow personally responsible for this depraved situation; I must be condemned and vile. And, of course, I could tell no one.

So, my father, who was appointed by God to protect me as his child, had cast me into the arms of a strange man in the middle of the night, opening my soul to the curse of sexual debauchery. For many long years I carried this secret burden of false guilt, abasement and shame inside myself. This went unchecked until the day that Jesus, my Saviour, came into my life and cleansed and purified and healed me.

Such was the world in which I grew up, and in which I tasted the bitter lessons of life. Through my wounded eyes, the adults around me became fountains of pain. My view of myself plummeted lower and lower as the years went by. The gashes and incurable wounds in my heart grew more deep and raw.

The things people around me strove after and most highly valued were money, power, pride, and position in society. I had inherited none of those advantages. To escape my world and gain them on my own, I resolved that I would become famous and successful, no matter what it cost. A desperate determination was birthed to show everyone – even myself – that I was actually worth something. Then, people would love me and I would be satisfied and happy. If I could achieve this, I would attain safety and security in this world, and I might be able to use my wealth to help others who were in need.

I had always been interested in spiritual things. When I was a young girl, I dreamed a strange and very vivid dream. In the dream, I stood on the sport's field next to our school. Suddenly, on the small hill next to the field I saw a gigantic white pillar reaching up to heaven. I didn't move, but suddenly I was next to this pillar, and in my dream I knew that the pillar was the Eternal One. I don't remember whether he said anything to me, but what I do remember is the experience of unearthly awe, mixed with holy reverence and trembling. I felt a strong sense of unworthiness, lostness, and the hopeless smallness of my humanity.

I think it was in that moment that I first understood how fearsome it is to be in the presence of the holiness of God. A huge gap stood between him and me. I was infinitely far from him, even though in the dream he was right beside me. From this I felt terribly sad, as if I were estranged from something most precious and valuable. The overwhelming emotions of that dream were so real that, even after so many years, remembering the dream still evokes those same strong feelings.

When I awoke, I called out that I had seen God in a dream. My grandmother began to question me as to what God was like and what he said, but I didn't know how to answer. From that time on I carried some kind of 'spiritual holy fear', as I called it. It is possible that in the mercy of God this spurred my earnest spiritual search in the years that followed.

There was no mosque in our village in those Soviet days, but after this I stayed close to my mother so that I could imitate her in the prayer rituals, holy days and other practices of our religion. She took me to visit the graves of our ancestors and various holy places. I watched her care for my grandparents, give to orphans and the poor, and help the elderly. These acts were the only way I knew to be close to God.

My grandmother frequently read the Koran, the holy book of Islam, and would tell us Islamic religious stories. When I grew older, I was drawn to religious literature. I observed the Muslim fasts and the regular Muslim prayers. Time after time I tried to fulfil the religious precepts of Islam, hoping that in so doing I would find peace with my Creator and peace in my heart.

On the other hand, I didn't understand God. Sometimes I accused and blamed him, but I very much wanted to know God. This thirst for God within me and spiritual hunger only intensified over the course of time. It seemed that disillusionment in life and religion, on one side, and my interest towards the Most High, on the other side, were increasing within me simultaneously. In my inner being there was something that made me feel that perhaps all the religious activities were just products of human fiction. I was not sure and did not speak about it out loud, but I thought and wanted something more.

Although there were moments when I doubted the existence of Allah, for the most part I firmly believed that *he is*.

Situations arose in my life where, based on the facts, I should have died, and only the Eternal God could have saved me. He actually did save me more than once. In the middle of all the painful things, I saw God's hand on my life in many ways, starting from childhood.

2

Twisted 'Love'

For as long as I can remember, I have always loved to sing. It seems to me I was probably born singing because I have no memories of ever living without it. Singing to me was like breathing. I sang everywhere and all the time. Whatever I was doing, wherever I was, I could always hear music inside me. Music became my comfort, my joy, and it was music that in the saddest moments of my life gave me hope for a better future.

Whenever our community gathered, whether for a wedding or a birthday, a welcome or farewell, or even building a house or working in the fields, there was always dancing, singing and story-telling. Someone inevitably called out, 'Oh, Shaadia,[1] please sing for us!' I was very shy, and when I was in front of people it was difficult for me to actually open my mouth – but once I started to sing, all timidity vanished, and I became totally immersed in my music.

From an early age, I participated in singing competitions – in the local school, the cultural club, and in my region. I regularly won top prizes. Even as a very little girl, I was almost always summoned back to the stage for an encore. I had every hope of achieving my goal of fame and riches by singing.

Praise and honours came my way. But for me, the greatest reward and honour was when my father – from whom you never heard even one positive word – occasionally praised my singing. I could not tell you where my certificates and awards are; I don't even remember what most of them look like. But I will never forget the day when I was performing a song on the stage, and saw at the far end of the hall my half-drunk father. At first I was frightened when I saw that he was speaking to someone and pointing at me. But when I discovered that he was boasting to his friends about how well his daughter sang, my joy and amazement knew no bounds. The fact that my father was proud of me and openly praising me to others was absolutely stunning, phenomenal, like something out of a fairy tale!

There was no financial support for my education after high school. I applied to several musical training schools but my efforts always came to a dead end, partly because I had no formal musical education and I could not play an instrument. In addition, my Russian language skills were poor, and I was overwhelmingly shy. But at the age of eighteen I went to Moscow in search of a better life.

Rosy dreams and fairy-tale expectations filled my mind and heart as I made this first journey beyond the borders of my home region. I was a teenager, a simple village girl, naive and gullible. My imagination was shaped by romantic novels and melodramatic Indian films, so different from the negative atmosphere in which I had grown up. My expectations were distorted, to say the least.

I got a job in a state kindergarten. The salary was very small, but lots of courses and youth activities were available in the evenings at accessible rates. I studied ballroom dancing and speed-reading, English, sewing, and other subjects. I also became one of the Komsomol (All-Union Leninist Young

Communist League) leaders in our organization: the kindergarten belonged to the Ministry of Internal Affairs of Russia. But quite rapidly the rosy clouds of my romantic expectations faded into painful realities.

At home as a teen I had no shortage of male admirers – men often told me they were in love with me – but I was full of unexpressed emotional and psychological confusion and stress. In school, I was held up as an example of 'a most modest, proper young woman', but this 'proper' façade was a screen covering serious emotional problems.

If my father had had even the slightest thought that one of his daughters might be conversing with a member of the opposite sex, he would have ascribed to that simple conversation extreme sexual misbehaviour. Our culture placed high demands on females for modesty and restraint while males, it seemed, were given permission to do practically anything – and were even honoured for their exploits. A young woman who was the victim of sexual violence was normally blamed and accused. Consequently, I grew up with a complete lack of positive patterns for relationships with the opposite sex, and instead, carried a mass of emotional complexes, unhealthy fears and misrepresentations.

My self-image was terrible. My mother, though kind, was not able to teach us girls much because she herself was so beaten down and unhappy. My father's 'parental training' consisted of violent threats and curses, which often descended into beating us with a shepherd's crook. My childhood and teen years had a complete absence of positive examples or instruction about how to build respectful relationships, and a devastating deficit of security and self-protection. For me, entering into adult life, such a foundation did nothing to protect me or help me avoid evil. Quite the contrary.

I lived in a dormitory in Moscow. One evening in my third year, my friends and I celebrated the New Year holiday together. Everyone was in great spirits. A friend brought me some alcohol. 'You ought to try a little,' he said, 'in honour of the holiday. Just to know the kind of things that exist in the world.'

I had spent a lot of time with this young man. Although I learned later that others saw us as a future bride and groom, I had never considered marrying him. I was young and curious and interested in many things. I had no desire to obligate myself to lifelong family responsibilities – not yet. I was also naive and immature. My unhealthy sense of self-rejection, my craving for love and my extreme gullibility played major roles in what took place.

At the beginning of the evening everything was merry – so merry that I didn't notice when my mental processes began to cloud as my friend offered me tastes of drink after drink. I didn't notice the point when I crossed the fatal line after which you don't grasp much of anything. Only the following morning did I come to discover that something horrible had happened, something I had feared and which I had thought would never happen to me.

Shame filled me. How I wished it would turn out to be a nightmare! This was an 'un-erasable' stain that left little hope of a future marriage and happy family – on the wedding night in our culture, a reputable senior relative checks whether the bride is a virgin. If she is not, tradition requires that she is thrown out of the window. It is a huge shame for her, all her life. (The groom, however, can have had as many sexual partners as he wished!)

I tried to comfort myself with the thought, 'We will get married and everything will be OK. It isn't really that bad if he becomes my husband.'

But when my 'knight' announced with a triumphant smirk that I was overwhelmingly naive and gullible and he was happy he had made a conquest of me, I was beside myself with indignation. 'Now there is nowhere you can get away from me. No one else will take you as a wife. You will have to marry me.' So this was exactly what he had planned! This was how he loved me? I saw at once that he had set himself up in a powerful position over all other contenders with his horrible plan, not thinking even once about me or my feelings!

I exploded with rage. I hated him. I vividly expressed to him in the bluntest words my deeply held feelings. Even if he were the last man on the face of the earth, there was no way that I would ever consider marrying him. It was over. For me he had turned into a monstrous traitor.

The emotional blow was so great that I completely lost my voice. With my love for singing, this second tragedy was as devastating as the first. No matter how I tried, I could no longer sing. This one comfort, which always warmed my heart in the most difficult times, had been taken from me.

My heart was shattered. My whole life seemed destroyed. I had no value to anyone, for no one would marry a 'ruined' woman like me. The thought had been pounded into us from earliest childhood.

As the months and years followed, my life tumbled further and further down a rocky slope, resulting in greater and greater destruction and disillusionment. Feeling broken down inside, and with nothing to lose, and longing for love, I had further sexual relationships with men. How many times from my earliest childhood had I heard my father's drunken threats, 'I'll bury you alive!' or, 'I'll cut you up in pieces like cattle . . . if ever . . . '? Now I felt myself under those curses. All the 'if evers' had taken place; my life was irretrievably shameful and ruined. My father's voice constantly shouted in my mind all the merciless judgment that would rain down upon me. I was vulnerable, powerless and hopeless; nothing or no one could ever change my horrible life. Oh, how I wanted everything to be different!

I spoke to no one about any of this. The culture of shame and judgment was so powerful that it would not allow me to speak. All that was left was to lead a kind of double life of slavery to lies, fear, internal pain and despair, always outwardly wearing the 'mask'.

It sounded like a good plan. It was 1991 and I was headed home to the Caucasus, and it would be more convenient to spend the last couple of days before my departure in Moscow with friends from my home region. It would be much simpler to get to the airport the next day from their apartment, rather than from where I lived in an outlying district, further from Moscow.

As it turned out, on that same day, my friends were asked to share their place for two days with a group of four men also en route home to the Caucasus via Moscow. These four natives of my home region called themselves Muslims and outwardly presented themselves as respectable. They had been working somewhere in the far north of Russia.

This particular evening my friends were both working a second shift and so they would be away till after midnight.

To do some drinking at the table was usual for most men from the Caucasus then. In keeping with Caucasus tradition, as the only woman in the home, I played the role of hostess. In the absence of my host friends, I prepared a meal and politely served the men at the table while they ate and drank. Before long the alcohol had an impact on their brains. They tried to convince me to drink a little with them. I had no interest in this, and with difficulty, hiding my revulsion at male intoxication, I politely refused. Too many times of suffering in my life were connected with male drunkenness.

Drunken men themselves were repulsive and loathsome to me and stirred up fear verging on panic. The oldest of the four men was especially offensive. He kept physically trying to force me to drink vodka. I don't know how it happened but I lost control and spat it directly into his face. The men were furious. They seemed to be only waiting for something like this to happen. They grabbed me and threw me into a back room, saying that they would each rape me in revenge.

I had never expected anything like this at the hands of my countrymen, especially when they had been warmly welcomed into the home of our mutual friends. Sitting in that back room I quickly set aside my anger and started thinking how I could get out of this dilemma. My friends would not be home from work any time soon. There wasn't anyone who could help me.

I don't know where I found the cool-headed composure, but I reckoned that fighting, tears, or pleading would do me no good. When they brought me back to the group I started playing up to them. At the first opportunity, I leapt out of the apartment. Since it was bitterly cold outside, I ran up the inside stairway to the second floor and down that hallway. At the first apartment, I urgently rang the buzzer. I was thrilled when a man and woman together opened the door. But when they looked past me and saw four Caucasus men sprinting towards me down the hall, they immediately slammed the door and disappeared. I felt like a helpless, doomed lamb surrounded by a pack of merciless wolves.

These men, who had allowed alcohol to transform them into wild beasts, came after their prey, grabbing their unfortunate victim, hauling me back to the apartment, where they ripped off all my clothes. They started planning a group sexual orgy as 'punishment' for my offences.

In that moment I called out to God from the depths of my heart to save me, if he existed and could hear me. At the same time I sought to delay in every way that I could, in the hope of finding some way of outwitting these would-be rapists.

The leader completely undressed. Everything about his body and appearance summoned total horror and revulsion in me. The other three, who were also mostly undressed, sat around in a circle, each waiting his turn. I was in despair, but with all my strength I tried not to let it show. I refused to show any fear in front of this slime.

My brain worked feverishly as in my heart I kept crying out to the Most High. And then a miracle began to unfold. The leader, who no longer even seemed human to me, suddenly became extremely nervous. Out of some kind of timidity, he requested the rest of the guys to go into another room and leave him alone with me. Hope started to rise. One man was better than four. After the other three went out, the man looked around for his cigarettes. I seized the moment and told him I had seen his cigs in the kitchen.

'You go and get them,' I said. 'I'll just wait here.'

What I needed was for him to go out of the room, even for a moment. My only hope was a few seconds when I could spring for the window and try to get it open. Right then it was irrelevant to me that it was at least twenty degrees Celsius below zero (-5 Fahrenheit) and I was without clothes. The main thing was – would the window open? This apartment was on the first floor. In Moscow, apartment windows were typically nailed shut in winter or glued shut to keep out the cold. But the window was my last hope. The very second that the man went into the kitchen, I leapt for the window. I found myself outside, running I didn't know where.

It was late at night. The street was empty. I wore nothing but the slippers on my feet as I ran over the snow in the freezing cold. Whether from shock or the joy of having escaped that horror, I didn't even feel the cold. As I came to my senses, I realized that I was in danger of falling into even worse danger – or death.

I decided to go towards the next apartment building. All entry doors in Moscow apartments are electronically locked and need a special entry code to get in. Just then I heard the beep of someone opening an entry door. Peeking around the corner of the building, I saw a man going in the door closest to where I was hiding. He hadn't seen me, and I prayed that somehow the door would not close tightly behind him.

It didn't.

I waited until the sound of his footsteps faded inside. Then I sprang through the door and up the stairs of the tall building. I ran as if I were out of my mind. As I neared the top of the long stairway, I started feeling the cold and knew I was going to need human help.

I knocked on the closest apartment door. A middle-aged man opened it. When he saw this young woman – naked – his face turned all sorts of colours of shock and disbelief, and he slammed the door.

I knocked on the next door. To my overwhelming thankfulness, a grey-haired older woman opened the door. With a warm spirit and even a touch of good-natured humour, she welcomed me into her apartment. When I began to tell her that her next-door neighbour would not help me, a young person in desperate need, she chuckled. She told me this neighbour had been a bachelor all his life and had a deep fear of women. So now, in the middle of the night, a young woman dressed only in slippers knocking at his door? He would probably wonder for the rest of his life how that had happened!

This woman kindly gave me clothing and put me into her bed to warm up. She fed me hot tea with honey and raspberry sauce. I told her what had happened, and she showed so much compassion, understanding and love that I finally began to relax. But when I relaxed, I went into uncontrollable hysterics. This loving woman tried to comfort me. She named me a 'female hero' – a delicate girl triumphing over four grown men. As she talked, I realized how much I hated those men. From the depths of my soul, I wanted the most horrible and brutal sufferings to come to them.

I telephoned my friends, and they came for me after they had returned home from work. Their apartment was in total chaos. Everything had been flung around and turned upside down, but the men were gone. My friends were enraged at what these men had done.

It took me a long time to come to myself after this experience. I could not look at men without revulsion and hate. Forgive me, dear male readers, but at that time I was not capable of distinguishing between that type of man and any other. For me, all were the same. I winced when a person of the opposite sex even touched me accidentally. Images from that night ran constantly before my eyes and made me nauseous.

3

False 'Love'

That last night in Moscow could have been much worse. God had heard my cry and intervened in the situation to save me from further devastation. But in my head, a battle went back and forth. On the one hand, I saw the evidence of divine intervention on my behalf: the window which so easily and quickly opened, the entry door at the other building which stayed open for me, the kind lady who took me into her apartment and helped me . . . All of this together could not have been chance. Even that I didn't freeze or become sick from the bitter cold was a wonder to me. On the other hand, I was wounded and offended. Couldn't God in his power have kept this demeaning experience from happening to me? Maybe he didn't love me! I felt alone and unhappy.

And I still couldn't sing. I couldn't wash my troubled soul with music as I always had before. My need to sing was so strong that I felt it physically in my chest.

After I lost my voice, the inner need to sing seemed to grow even stronger until it became overwhelming. I went through a period of deep emotional suffering and depression. Surely this ended my hopes for a singing career, and my life. However, at this lowest point something else deep inside me cried out. The smallest sliver of hope rose in my heart. I *would* see my voice return. I *would* sing, no matter what the cost. Despite the diagnoses of doctors and specialists, I simply could not reconcile myself to the conclusion that I would never sing again.

During the years in Moscow I came to understand that without singing and without my dream of the stage, I simply could not live; and so I decided with great determination that I would return to performing and in so doing bury my pain and sadness and gain happiness in life.

In the Soviet days, there was no such thing as unemployment. In fact, it was against the law not to work, but by the 1990s all that had changed. I was able to quit my job, which I didn't like much anyway, and return to my home region to pursue my dreams. And so, I moved alone to Temer-Kala, the capital city of my home region near the Caspian Sea, with no money, and no helpful connections to assist me in accomplishing my dream. But I was bold and stubborn and refused to give up.

Learning to sing again demanded unbelievable effort, will-power, stubbornness and perseverance. Where before I had sung like a nightingale without thinking about it, now I needed medical treatments for my vocal chords, and countless voice lessons. But I had set myself an unshakeable goal, and I was full of enthusiasm and undaunted faith that I would achieve success. No one could stop me.

The sober reality was that no one believed in me. No one who knew me believed that my voice could be restored, or that I could become a professional singer. Voice specialists, with whom I consulted, said I would never restore my singing voice; I should forget about singing. But after all I had been through, this goal had become the one thing in which I saw meaning in my life. For me it was a question of life and death. So I took hold of my hoped-for singing career just as a drowning person latches onto the last piece of wood on the sea. Difficulties only increased my enthusiasm and strengthened my resolve to show everyone what I was worth.

Then I met with the chief musician of the National Philharmonic orchestra. It turned out that he had just had a fight with his girlfriend, and there I was – young, beautiful and promising! He decided to take me along with his team to the international folk music festival which was held in the Netherlands. At that time – in the early 1990s – foreign travel was still very prestigious for Russians. So this was incredibly lucky for me. For him, it was an opportunity to take revenge on his wayward lover! Of course, he had some hope of an intimate relationship with me. That did not happen. But he was still very sympathetic towards me and helped me a lot. Composers and some of the very best musicians helped me, too. I was very outgoing in spite of the brokenness inside, and for me it was easy to build friendly relationships with people. Relationships are very important in our culture.

Therefore, although it was impossible to believe that I would be able to restore my voice to its former state, people began to see my commitment, and to wish me well. But there was also a great deal of envy.

At the beginning, none of my relatives supported me. My sisters were offended. They indignantly proclaimed that a female singer was no more than a woman of ill repute. Indeed, I constantly had to fight off predatory males. In our society, they considered female singers as easy prey, tasty unprotected morsels to consume. My brother said it was foolish to hope that I could become a successful singer, especially since I was already twenty-six years old. They loved me in their own way and wanted only good, but at the time these family responses were painful and wounding.

The only person who encouraged me and gave me moral support was my mother. She told me that before I sang publicly, I must be certain that I would work to become one of the very best singers – otherwise, it would be better to not even start. I received her advice and wisdom with deep thankfulness. That year, 1993, I entered the local state university and later graduated with a degree in cultural studies.

Looking back, I am amazed at myself. On the one hand I was full of emotional pain, internal fears, and extreme timidity. On the other, I found within me raw courage to the point of audacity, along with a streak of unwavering determination and stubbornness. Any mountain in front of me would just have to move. That attitude was a shocking contrast to the young woman so full of pain and fear. I resolved that no power would block me from whatever goal I set before me. I believed with all my heart, 'If you strongly set your heart on something, anything is possible.'

One day, early in my musical efforts, I was working on one of my first recordings in a small, humble recording studio. At that moment a well-known leader of a popular TV music programme stuck his head into my little recording room. He was highly respected and often helped young musical talent out of genuine caring and good-heartedness. From that chance meeting, a warm relationship began, and he invited me to perform at a New Year concert called 'Blue Fire' on regional television.

I couldn't believe it! I told all my friends about my upcoming television performance. However, being the fearful and self-critical person that I was, when I watched the final recording, I was terribly upset. I thought it was a disaster. I didn't want anybody to see it. You can imagine my shock and amazement when people began to congratulate me and praise my singing. The morning after my performance was aired, I woke up famous!

One of my professors at university was extremely strict and laid down severe consequences to any student late to class. We all feared him. On the first day of classes after the New Year holiday, I was five minutes late. I was terrified as I walked into the auditorium, but I heard no agitation or rebuke. Instead, the professor exclaimed with a big smile, 'That was terrific! That was awesome!'

What was he talking about? Was I going crazy? Finally some of my classmates helped me to understand he was praising my TV performance. That programme represented the beginning of my success on the musical stage.

That same year I gave my debut solo performance in a large concert hall. To the consternation of my sceptics and antagonists, the concert was a resounding success. During the holidays, I organized my first musical concert tour through towns and villages of our region. I was administrator, sound manager, and lead singer, all three! Some called me an 'impudent upstart', and were openly indignant about my confidence. Any success they attributed to my 'looks', inferring that I was an untalented 'baby doll'. Sometimes the attacks cut deeply; more than once I was reduced to floods of tears; but my determination only intensified.

Others praised my hard-working perseverance, musical talent, and even my intelligence. This encouraged me. Over the course of time, such words of honour gradually increased. I resolutely pressed forward, holding fast to my dream of great success and the goal of living a life with meaning.

Of course, I committed many major mistakes, and learned a lot in the process. I felt I was constantly tackling endless difficulties and seemingly insurmountable obstacles on this road to my goal. The restoration of my voice was a long and difficult process. During that period, my voice wasn't completely restored, but I made a lot of progress. I used to sing folk and popular songs in my native Avar language. (Now I sing only within the framework of Christian ministry.)

By the mid-1990s I achieved a level of fame as a singer, began to earn a lot of money, and gained the love and respect of fans and followers. Judging by outward appearances, everything was going well. I was proud that I had achieved this summit of fame and money by my own efforts, but something important was missing inwardly and this bothered me more and more. I had an insatiable hunger for purity and holiness, and was constantly grieved that I could see no way of satisfying this longing. On the way to success I tasted the bitterness and ugliness of envy, jealousy, power struggles, slander, hypocrisy, greed and sexual immorality.

At first I felt like a naive victim of all this ugliness, but I soon became infected with the same diseased way of life. Yes, I was naive, but I was also foolish because, before long, I learned these same behaviours and repeated them myself, often almost unconsciously. It seemed that I had to function this way just to survive. Sin spreads like a flu virus, and I did nothing to prevent the illness from destroying me. I deceived myself and ended up in despair and disillusionment. Yes, I had become famous and achieved worldly success, but I had not found real love, internal peace, cleanness in my soul, or the honest happiness which I had sought. The love that this world presented to me brought even greater pain and melancholy and took me to even deeper levels of loneliness and despair.

During those years a lot of powerful men proclaimed their love to me. For a while, life took on bright colours and I felt beautiful. These episodes always started full of beauty and romance. And they always ended with emptiness and disillusionment. As if to avenge my pitiful attempts at happiness, loneliness fastened its deadly claws around my throat and squeezed ever tighter. I felt like the person lost in the desert, dying from thirst, but the mirage I chased with my dying strength always turned out to be barren sand.

Again and again, with frightful naivety, I grabbed on to what looked like love, but was left totally disappointed and in pain, wanting only one thing – to die. Hurt, bitterness, guilt and a growing sense of personal unworthiness increasingly left me bereft of joy or strength. I had fallen into a quagmire and was doomed to die. This hellish circle I lived in had no exit; it would strangle me. I hated myself and my life.

In all the world, I could trust no one – not even myself. More and more I felt a dreadful emptiness and sense of total meaningless in life. Despite a sea of fans, money and beautiful friends, I couldn't escape this horrifying feeling of loneliness and deadness that held my spirit in icy shackles. Ultimately I had to admit that I had just created a beautiful facade, no more than fig leaves to cover my nakedness. Behind this facade lived someone that no one knew – a lonely and unhappy little girl, desperately in need of love, pure, simple, genuine and unconditional.

Outwardly I continued to present a glittering masquerade of 'superstar', idol of many, subject of envy and gossip, while inside I was completely disillusioned and empty. Everything that I strove for with huge expenditure of energy, everything that at one time had seemed so desirable and valuable as the source of meaning and importance in life – alas! – turned out to hold no real meaning at all. Even worse – it seemed pitiful. I didn't want to keep living, and often went to bed at night with the hope that I would go to sleep and never wake up again.

In those days, I was mixing in influential circles with those who held both government authority and Mafia-like illegal power in my region. The wealthy husband of my youngest sister was a strong athlete and a powerful underworld figure. I was not intimidated by him, and so he hated me. At the same time my sister was suffering terribly from his mistreatment of her. I have to admit that it crossed my mind to consider whether some underworld friend of mine could have him killed.

This brother-in-law was extremely shrewd, feared no one, and would often fall into dark moods where he became brutal and wildly out of control. Everyone feared him. I was determined to save my sister from his influence, and to do whatever it took to achieve this. Praise to the Lord! Even in my ignorance, he protected me. In his mercy, he stopped me from that violent deed and changed my hateful, vengeful heart.

Things calmed down, but nonetheless this brother-in-law saw me as a threat. And so he manufactured some slander about me for the purpose of getting me killed. My brother-in-law said that he saw me acting as a prostitute at a prestigious hotel. That was utter fiction. But he didn't want to just dishonour and destroy me – he wanted to have it done at the hands of my own blood relatives.

Incited by him, my brother and male cousins accused me of sexual transgression. By the customs of our culture they needed to kill me to preserve the honour of the men of our family. These men who were blinded by this hateful slander seemed to have forgotten that they were far from innocent and deserved the judgment of God as much as anybody.

False religions and false teachings often lead people into the most awful errors and ugliness from the depths of hell itself. What kind of righteousness or honour is this, if those judging another are guilty of the same or worse evil themselves? What could be worse than murdering another human being? Only God is the Creator of human life; the one who gives us life. Those who take another's life are battling against the Creator himself. The devil does everything he can to blind the eyes and the minds of people to accomplish his 'steal, kill, destroy' purposes in the name of 'honour'.

I was terrified. I personally knew of cases where women in similar situations were murdered. And now I myself was right on the precipice of such a death. From childhood my father had constantly uttered violent threats about how he would bury us alive or cut us in pieces like butchered animals if ever he heard something foul about one of us. Our fatherly 'training' as daughters consisted basically of insults and violent threats regarding any misbehaviours with the opposite sex. I knew that my male relatives would talk with my father, and that would be the end for me.

One of my brother's closest friends (someone's friend becomes close to his whole family) warned me about this horrible plan. This friend was a kind-hearted, decent man and may God bless him and honour him for this. I went into hiding for several days with some friends. If you have never been in this kind of situation, it's hard to describe how it feels. It must be the way an animal would feel surrounded by a band of converging hunters, with no way of escape. After a number of days I decided that I had to do something because I couldn't go on like this. The only idea I had was to risk finding my brother and trying to talk with him. After all, I thought, 'My brother is an intelligent and educated person; it just can't be that he supports such a barbaric plan against his sister!'

I reached him first by telephone, and then we actually met. I came back from Moscow to my home region, feeling like a criminal.

And, glory to God, this nightmare did end positively.

Only later did I learn from my sister that my brother and male cousins had gone to see my father. They told him about their plans and wanted his agreement, but to their surprise (and my amazement and joy) my father's response was not as they expected. He exploded in rage, told them off like stupid little boys, and threw them out of his house. He warned them that if they knew what was good for them, they had better not harm me. 'You're not even worthy to sit at the same table as her!' he yelled, according to my sister who was present.

How could I even begin to assimilate this stunning act by my father? I was in shock. His response was totally opposite to the violent threats I had endured from his mouth since childhood. I was overjoyed beyond words that my father, who had always been a source of fear to me, had actually risen to my defence at such a critical moment. It felt like a miracle. Thoughts of 'how much my father loved me' were completely unfamiliar in my soul, but this episode was like a healing balm to the wounds within me. A corner of my soul gave birth to warm feelings and gratefulness regarding the true heart of my father. At that time I thought to myself, 'I guess I never really knew him.'

Again, it was like a miracle from the Most High. Now I can say he truly saved me through so many dangers so that I could become one day the living testimony for him. Some girls were murdered in this way! From my childhood, I would hear time after time stories about women being murdered and buried by their brothers or father for fornication. Sometimes, afterwards it proved to be just slander. Such stories horrified me.

Whoever digs a pit will fall into it; if someone rolls a stone, it will roll back on them.

Proverbs 26:27

Today I am really saddened that my youngest sister's former husband, the one who tried to have me killed, was himself murdered a short time later, along with one of his brothers. If only I had then known the Saviour, who had already paid for everyone's sin. How great the mercy, love and forgiveness of God! After I came to know Christ and my eyes were opened, I truly mourned the loss of this talented young man. How I longed for his soul to have been saved for eternity! Also, his life is long past, and the hidden things belong to God.

> Say to them, 'As surely as I live, declares the Sovereign LORD, I take no pleasure in the death of the wicked, but rather that they turn from their ways and live. Turn! Turn from your evil ways! Why will you die, people of Israel?'
>
> Ezekiel 33:11

One night in the year following the murder plot against me, there was a gentle knock on my window. I recognized a close relative of my youngest sister's husband. This brother-in-law by that time had already been killed. The relative said through the window that he had some urgent news for me and could I step out for a minute? I was not afraid of this relative and thought I should find out what was going on. Since it was night-time, he asked me to sit in his car and he would bring me up to date on some important news. As soon as I got in the car, the driver suddenly accelerated and I noticed that there were other young men in the car also. They told me to sit quietly, not to move or make a sound.

Just like that I became the hostage of a group of young men. They drove me through the night to a village where they put me in the back room of a house, and set up a careful guard. These men were close relatives of the dead brother-in-law.

The matter revolved around money. There was a significant financial inheritance connected with this deceased brother-in-law, which by rights was to go to my sister and their son. But some of his relatives wanted the money for themselves. They decided to go after it in this vile manner, kidnapping me for leverage to get the money. I didn't even know what was going on.

As soon as my brother found out about this, he took action. He rounded up a circle of powerful friends from a band of armed men, who were like an underworld posse. In the face of this threat, the gambit of my kidnappers fell apart. I was released. I was probably held for twenty-four or thirty-six hours. Later, one of my sisters told me she had never seen my brother as upset as when he found out I had been taken hostage. He turned grey right before their eyes. He kept saying all night long that he would destroy anyone who did the slightest harm to me. It was a matter of honour for him as a man. What those men did to his sister was a humiliation for him, first of all. That was why he was furious. Of course, he also loved me as his sister.

Nevertheless, my relationship with my brother was seriously ruined by his earlier plotting against my life. In my stubborn and bull-headed pride, I could not forgive him for not protecting me from the ugly slander of the murder plot. The wounding and offence was so big for me that I could hardly bring myself to speak with him – not even when he rescued me from the kidnappers – not until some years after I came to Jesus. The Lord is the one who set me free from all sorts of wrong patterns in my heart and in my life. Today I love and respect my brother and am thankful to him for so much. True love triumphs over everything. Only Jesus can help a person to see everything in the true light.

I continued to observe the Muslim prayers and other religious rituals. I knew no other option. I was trying to prove to myself that all of this was good and right . . . and that *I* could be good and right. I was afraid of being spiritually disappointed, but to be perfectly honest, although I continued the Islamic prayers and other rituals, I didn't find a lot of meaning in them. More and more earnestly I asked Allah to show me his genuine truth. Every night I went to sleep with that prayer on my lips.

During that time, I started actively studying psychology. I read many books and dreamed of one day opening a psychological treatment centre where I could help those who were experiencing difficulties. I had experienced a lot myself; as a result, I thought I would be able to understand and help others. Often I *was* somewhat helpful to others, but I couldn't find any help for the darkness inside me.

I planned to study the Koran more seriously, hoping to find in Islam a relationship with the great Creator who had given me life. I wanted to know him personally and fully with all my heart, whatever it took. What I didn't want was to blindly follow him and bow down to what I didn't understand. I longed to believe that I wasn't just a random accident in this world but that there was some purpose and meaning to my life. I so much wanted to believe that the Eternal God existed and that he was loving, forgiving, kind and truly caring – not a distant, harsh, bloodthirsty judge.

The deeper I dug into religion and the more closely I adhered to religious activities, the more disillusioned I became. Islamic history made me wonder if I would ever find the kind of God that I hoped for. Maybe a God who was loving, forgiving, kind and caring didn't exist in Islam. This worried me.

As I write this, I deeply desire for you to understand my heart. At no time and in no way am I speaking against people – each person is individually precious – including those who follow the path of Islam. To speak against people would run completely contrary to my faith. This is simply my story. Islam itself was not the cause of my problem; it was my estrangement from my loving Creator and Saviour. It wouldn't have mattered what religion or philosophy I leaned on. The blunt truth was that I was personally lost. I will never cease to testify to how the Lord rescued me and performed miracles of grace and power in my life. As a result, I can only describe my personal journey – my search – and share with you the life-giving truth that I have found.

There are many wonderful, remarkable people among my Muslim friends, and I love them very much. The qualities of hospitality, generosity, sincerity and kindness, which are widespread in my home culture, find resonance with what our loving Creator calls for in his holy Word, the Bible.

But it would be dishonest not to acknowledge that more than once I have seen the most peaceful, good-hearted and generous of these friends become viciously hostile and extremely intolerant under the influence of severe religious principles. Such religion can completely blind the eyes and minds of ordinary people, pushing them into all sorts of folly, sowing seeds of fear, enmity and hatred.

Jesus said, 'The time is coming when anyone who kills you will think they are offering a service to God. They will do such things because they have not known the Father or me' (John 16:2,3). There is the key! Not knowing either the Father or Jesus! It is easy to follow rituals, traditions, or severe 'laws', zealously demanding obedience even with the threat of death, and then console oneself with the thought that we are serving God. But true faith demands knowledge and a living relationship with God, turning away from self and being filled with his unconditional love.

During the time of the Russian tsars, near the end of the nineteenth century, my great-grandfather was a highly honoured Muslim leader, considered to have great religious authority in his day – but he killed his own sister. She had dared to comb her hair on the veranda where others might see her. According to his understanding of Sharia law, this was unacceptable. My great-grandfather grabbed his sister by the hair so violently that he pulled a huge clump right out of her scalp. As a result of the injury, she got weaker and weaker and died.

The fate of his own wife was not much better. His brutal behaviour due to his religious zeal crippled one of his daughters, and caused his son (my grandfather) to become an invalid. My grandfather died at the age of thirty-three.

'He was just trying to sincerely enforce religious laws,' people say in my home culture – if they dare to speak about it at all. Fear and prejudice controls them.

> Woe to those who call evil good and good evil, who put darkness for light and light for darkness, who put bitter for sweet and sweet for bitter.
>
> Isaiah 5:20

> Watch out for false prophets. They come to you in sheep's clothing, but inwardly they are ferocious wolves. By their fruit you will recognise them. Do people pick grapes from thorn-bushes, or figs from thistles? Likewise, every good tree bears good fruit, but a bad tree bears bad fruit. A good tree cannot bear bad fruit, and a bad tree cannot bear good fruit. Every tree that does not bear good fruit is cut down and thrown into the fire. Thus, by their fruit you will recognise them.
>
> Matthew 7:15–20

Nonetheless, by Islamic standards, my ancestors were highly respected and devoted Muslims. One of my grandfathers was a Muslim holy man. A mosque was constructed over his grave and became a place where Muslims came to worship Allah. I have observed many times people refusing to respond to salvation because of their ancestors. 'If my ancestors went to hell, then I will go there with them. I will never betray the religion of my ancestors.' The 'Cult of Ancestors' is very strong in the culture in which I grew up. But the Holy Writings say that every person will give account to God himself (see Romans 14:12) – not their ancestors – for their own life and eternal destiny. I must choose for myself. Personally, I don't want my first loyalty to be to some kind of religion, philosophical system, or to people who are dead. I want to know my holy, eternal, living God and Creator and be faithful to him alone.

It boils down to a difference between a dry and hypocritical human religion on the one hand, or a living partnership of love and trust with your Creator on the other. A healthy vibrant partnership is possible only on the basis of freely chosen love and trust, not some blind, dead submission. Could I have this kind of living relationship with my Creator?

In light of my family's religious history, all sorts of doors in society were open to me at this time. I could develop a sparkling career, combining religion, psychology and music. But I wasn't seeking a new career. I had already achieved a successful public career, and it hadn't made me happy. I needed to find something that filled the emptiness inside me and brought real purpose to my earthly existence. Life was too short to waste on something false, meaningless, or ultimately worthless.

For everyone who asks receives; the one who seeks finds; and to the one who knocks, the door will be opened.

Matthew 7:8

I believed that I could only be loved, satisfied and happy if I become wealthy, famous, and powerful in society. If I achieved this, I would be safe and secure in this world, and I might even be able to use my wealth to help others who were in need.

But this path to success kept leading me into a place of even greater disillusionment. The emptiness inside me and the utter feeling of aloneness became greater and greater until they were virtually unbearable. Having reached this illusory summit of my lifetime goals, I realized that all of this was only a futile pursuit after something real – a clean, pure, non-hypocritical love. This genuine, pure love was the only thing that would fill the horrible emptiness inside me. I began to understand that this kind of pure love that I craved was not going to be found in the world full of hypocrisy and power struggle in which I then lived. Somewhere, somehow there had to be something completely good and pure – something that could not be bought with money or gained by struggle, the pure thing that would fill up this gaping deficit in human life. Without this, all I saw was isolation, disappointment, nameless melancholy, powerlessness, lostness, fear and grinding dissatisfaction. But what was it? And where was it?

I found no answers to my tormenting questions. Life became a heavier and heavier weight to me. Increasingly I thought about death as the only solution for my deliverance. I was so deadened that it didn't even particularly frighten me that people always said that those who commit suicide go to hell.

In those days I didn't have any clear picture of hell, and I thought, 'What difference would death make, since life on this earth is so much hell already?' I even remember how one very famous and literate cultural leader in the capital city of my region joked, 'In heaven, of course, everything will be beautiful and comfortable, but hell will be much more interesting because there you'll find so many of the most talented and fascinating people.' This was regarded by listeners as brilliant and funny. At that time I had no understanding of the reality of evil spiritual beings and the torment involved. Like this suave gentleman, I took death in a light-hearted fashion. How dreadfully deceived we were!

But there was something keeping me from killing myself. There had been a time previously, before I became a superstar, when I had seriously decided to commit suicide. I bought a pile of strong sleeping pills and prepared to leave this world which, for me, had become dead and cold. But at the last moment I suddenly saw a picture in front of me of my mother. She looked at me with such pain and despair in her eyes, and my determination wavered. I realized that I could not cause such enormous pain to her. My mother had suffered so much and had seen so little good in her existence; I could not inflict on her yet another cruel blow. Thus, I had to keep living out of regard for one person very dear to me who had suffered much more in life than I had. Ever since, although the thoughts of death visited me often (despite all my achievements) the picture of my mother kept me from actually committing suicide. But what was the point of my life? And how to even make any sense out of this disgusting earthly existence? I continued to search.

In the midst of all this, I believed in Allah, that is, the Eternal God, although I was experiencing more and more disappointment with religion in general.

In the late 1990s a man named Gadzhi appeared in my life at one of the most complex moments. He was powerful, manly and very wealthy. He had fallen in love with me, via my television performances, long before I met him. When he found out that one of his acquaintances was a long-time friend of mine, he promised to fulfil this friend's greatest life dream if he would only introduce Gadzhi to me.

At first I completely rebuffed his advances. I didn't want someone to buy me like a thing. Whenever someone started to woo me, I always instinctively resisted. The thought that someone with money would try to acquire me like an expensive doll was offensive. I wanted a genuine relationship of mutual respect, love and trust, not wealth! But eventually he captured my heart by his patient attentiveness, romantic kindnesses, and his generosity. When I saw the genuine spark of love in Gadzhi's eyes, my heart gradually yielded. In addition, I was so tired of the constant predatory attacks of various crude men around me, and he represented protection from all of that.

Within a few months I discovered I was pregnant. When eventually I told Gadzhi, he let me know that he was not happy. In his eyes, I was not destined for the birth of children. He had another woman for that purpose. My role to him was of an entirely different nature. In the depths of my soul, I couldn't reconcile myself to this diminished, truncated, unnatural role. I longed for a real relationship, not to be some kind of trophy or beautiful decoration for a man's pleasure and enjoyment. How had we concocted this grandiose sham under the name of 'love'?

I had not been planning to have a baby at that time, but when it happened I thought, 'Why not? Here it is!' I knew I eventually wanted children.

A few weeks went by, and Gadzhi's emotional state plummeted. To my horror, he aggressively demanded that I have an abortion. He insisted that I kill our unborn baby, whom I had already come to love and eagerly await. He would not call this baby 'ours', and refused to talk about the subject.

He constantly demanded that I get rid of 'it' as soon as possible. He assumed a hateful manner and threatened to publicly disgrace me. He threatened to turn me over to a gang of bandits to have me killed if I didn't take care of this. He was a powerful man, and I had seen what he was capable of when enraged.

I was terrified. I fell into deep despondency and couldn't understand anything. I felt demeaned and destroyed as a person. My lover had changed into a different person, constantly angry and unwilling to listen to a word I said. Even now I can't say exactly how I drove him to such rage, although I think it was due to someone placing doubts in his heart about my faithfulness. With the men in my culture, even the hint of such a thing would make them furious.

As I think back, I do not want to justify myself. I was as guilty as Gadzhi in a horrible sin. But at that time I considered myself a helpless victim, forced to abort my baby.

Unnatural birth in the sixth month of pregnancy! I felt like I was losing my mind. One day after a very painful conversation with Gadzhi, I went for a long walk through the city. I had completely lost any hope of saving the child's life. Feeling totally distressed, I kept saying as I walked, 'Forgive me, child. There's nothing else I can do.' My heart felt smashed from unbearable pain and I wanted to die.

For Gadzhi there was no higher authority above himself. No one and nothing could move him from his resolute determination. In his circle of men, the slightest sign of weakness was seen as a serious breakdown and could never be allowed. What a desperate, misleading delusion all this was and totally opposite to the character of the God I did not yet know!

Everything was accomplished through private channels, with a lot of money changing hands. Experiencing all this, I saw yet one more ugly sphere of reality in this world. It horrified me to see with my own eyes that every day in my city babies are heartlessly murdered – babies that were intended to be born into loving arms. Outwardly respectable-looking people do this business day after day while the rest of society gives wordless assent. Married women do this openly, often with no sense of shame, considering the legality of their marriage to be the only factor of significance, not the life of the innocent child they are prepared to brutally murder.

In the private channels 'underground' this same horrifying procedure was taking place with unmarried women concerned only that the pregnancy not be found out. 'Fig leaves' and 'masks' – how much evil they produce! The opinion of other people and the fear of human judgment become far more important than the life of a tiny and defenceless human being, or than respect and honour to the Creator God.

No one knew about my abortion. I had only spoken about it to one person – my closest girlfriend. I simply could not talk about this to anyone else. First of all, I was terrified by the violent threats from Gadzhi. Secondly, I did not want to cause pain to my mother. And, third, for me personally it would have been a huge disgrace and humiliation in a very wide circle because I was well-known to the public in my region of Russia.

A few days after the abortion I experienced severe internal bleeding. I was at home alone and lost so much blood that it was a miracle that I survived the night. In the midst of all this I went into a period of delirium and I couldn't be left alone. My friend came and stayed with me every night. We were trying to get me stabilized and healed without anyone knowing. Every night I had terrifying nightmares. I spent weeks trying to get myself back together emotionally and physically.

Almost immediately after this, dreadful things happened in Gadzhi's life. The close relative and good friend who had insisted upon the abortion was brutally murdered. Soon after, Gadzhi lost his position and power in the government and he had to go underground. His losses did not make anything easier for me, but that was what happened. God's law of sowing and reaping is constantly evident in human lives. Unless, of course, that person repents and entrusts themselves to the grace of God, the grace through Jesus which has already paid for our sins.

> Do not be deceived: God cannot be mocked. A man reaps what he sows. Whoever sows to please their flesh, from the flesh will reap destruction; whoever sows to please the Spirit, from the Spirit will reap eternal life.
>
> Galatians 6:7,8

On one of those nights when I was recovering, my friend could not be with me. At first I was worried as to how I would make it through the night, but later that evening, to my surprise, I felt more peaceful and fell soundly asleep. In the middle of the night I was awakened by these words, 'I will open before you many doors around the world. Don't be afraid of anything.' When I awoke I felt an awesome sense of peace and joy where for months and even years I had known none. It was a small word of hope in the midst of a painful time.

Part Two

Found

Ask and it will be given to you; seek and you will find; knock and the door will be opened to you.

Matthew 7:7

Now hope does not disappoint, because the love of God has been poured out in our hearts by the Holy Spirit who was given to us.

Romans 5:5 NKJV

4

Finding True Love

Longing for a living relationship with Allah, I prayed night after night before falling asleep: 'I don't really care what people think; I want to know what is pleasing to you – to live according to your will. If it is pleasing to you for me to continue with these religious rituals, I will do them all my life with joy. But if not, let me know. I want to know the true path.' Every night I waited for an answer.

One night, having fallen asleep with this prayer, I dreamed a vivid dream. In the dream, I continued to express this prayer to God. Suddenly I saw far off a vision of a very close friend of mine who had died several years before in a car accident. She looked at me and shook her head from side to side, repeating, 'No, Shaadia, no. It's not true; it's not correct.'

Waking, I knew that this was the Eternal God answering my question. Immediately I stopped all the Islamic religious rituals. They had no meaning for me, but it wasn't in my mind to turn away from Islam. I simply concluded that these outward activities weren't necessary for God. I continued to believe in God/Allah as I had before, but without all these rituals.

During these same months I ran into a long-time close friend, a well-known composer in our city of Temer-Kala. It had been two years since I had last seen him. At that time his family had been in the midst of crisis. His daughter Madina had lost her husband in a tragic accident. She was left to raise two young children on her own. I did not know Madina very well at the time, but I could see how emotionally devastated, dishevelled and hopeless she was. It was painful even to look at her.

I had thought of Madina several times over the years and wondered if she could even still be alive. Now, two years later when I met my composer friend again, I asked him about his daughter. He said she had not only recovered from her grief, but had been restored to full health and was living a joyful life full of success and well-being. She was thriving, heading up the business that had been left to her after the death of her husband.

I was amazed. More accurately, I was shocked and stunned. I vividly recalled the dispirited, dysfunctional person I had seen two years ago. Such a change seemed impossible. What could be the reason behind such an amazing transformation?

Over the next three months I could not get Madina's story out of my mind. Finally, I decided to visit this mysterious 'centre' where, according to her father, Madina's miraculous change had been effected. It must be some kind of psychological treatment centre, I thought. I convinced my youngest sister to go with me.

Having tried life accomplishments and religious activities without any real healing of my pain, psychological insight was my last hope. Although I didn't harbour any great illusions of perfect breakthroughs, in some way, a real person had been remarkably helped. So I set out to discover what methods they had used to bring about these surprising results for Madina. To my huge surprise, what I found was something completely and unexpectedly different.

When my sister and I arrived at the building, we walked into the main meeting room. Some type of worship service was underway. Honestly, it all seemed strange and weird to me and didn't result in a positive impression at all. I was suffering from a bad headache and just wanted this meeting, whatever it was, to be over as soon as possible. My sister tugged on me to go home, but my curiosity kept me a little longer, to see what else would happen. I can only give thanks to the Most High God for this grace which kept me.

The musical worship ended, and Bible preaching followed. Somehow this preacher seemed to know everything I was thinking and was aware of the exact questions bothering me. I listened with bated breath to every word. I forgot all else and drank in every word like parched ground absorbing drops of rain. Something strange started happening to me. My hands became extremely warm. This was particularly unusual in my case because my hands were always freezing cold. Besides, it was a cold winter day. I was sitting in the last row, hoping that no one would recognize me, the famous singer. My hands got so hot that I secretly tried to cool them on the cold wall behind me.

By the end of the preaching, I had a number of questions which I really wanted to ask the preacher. My sister waited while I almost ran forward to speak with this man who seemed to understand all my struggles. There was no point in trying to hide; it was evident that quite a few people in the meeting had already recognized me. Besides, I didn't want to hide. But the preacher sidestepped and avoided me. Maybe he was think-ing that I was one of those aggressive Muslims who sometimes came to Christian gatherings to attack believers. Thankfully, there were other people who were very ready and willing to converse with me.

In my country, there are more than forty ethnic groups, each with their completely unique language and culture. An Avar woman, someone of my own nationality, named Hadizhat, came up to me. I trusted her immediately because of her warm manner and the modest and godly way she was dressed, in my Muslim view. She told me her story, as did several others, and they made a deep impression. The entire atmosphere was one of unusual love, warmth, openness, joy and simplicity. This moved my heart powerfully. Everything contrasted with the world in which I was living. On the one hand, the outer attributes of this place were not impressive at all – cheap musical equipment, unprofessional musicians, a plain, unattractive meeting room. The people themselves had no splendid appearance or attire. Nothing carried any external attraction. But at the same time, there was some kind of internal power, confidence of spirit, internal joy in these people – all those things that were not in my glittering 'superstar' existence – and it turned my world upside down.

> The Spirit of the Lord is on me,
>> because he has anointed me
>> to proclaim good news to the poor.
> He has sent me to proclaim freedom for the prisoners
>> and recovery of sight for the blind,
> to set the oppressed free,
>> to proclaim the year of the Lord's favour.

Luke 4:18,19

I had landed in a completely new world, one previously unknown to me. This world drew me, called me. With greedy desire I drank in huge gulps of the long-sought sincerity, simplicity and purity. This was what I had been looking for – for years. I can't say that I immediately understood and fully responded. Of course, that wouldn't have been possible. I conversed with these people for a long time that day. Could I come from time to time and visit with them? 'Only without Jesus, because I am a Muslim and Mohammed is my Prophet.' (In Islam Jesus is understood as only a prophet. Any thought of his crucifixion and resurrection is totally out of the picture.)

My new friends answered that without Jesus, who died and rose again, any conversation would lose all meaning. It was only thanks to him and what he did on the cross that their lives had changed.

I was intrigued. In all my years in Islam, Mohammed had never changed my life even though I begged for spiritual help. How could Jesus change lives so amazingly? I decided that I would have to sort this out on my own.

I was amazed to meet so many people of Caucasian nationalities in this Christian meeting. All of them were former Muslims. I had always been told that it was Christians who turned to Islam, but here was a different reality.

It's not a simple thing to admit that everything you've been taught and believed since childhood isn't what you thought it was. It was like treasuring a diamond for years only to find out it was counterfeit. Then you discover you can exchange the counterfeit diamond for the genuine original! What healthy-thinking person would turn away from such an opportunity?

I decided to give it a look. I took a pile of books home with me that evening – books about Jesus, especially the Injil, the New Testament. I started reading and didn't stop until I had read the entire New Testament from beginning to end. This was 26 November 2000.

I didn't understand everything, but one thing I knew: I had found that which I had been seeking, and what I had found was summed up in one simple name – Jesus. For the first time I gained real hope that my burning thirst for genuine love, purity and holiness could be satisfied. My primary question – What was my purpose here on earth? – could be answered. And the answer was in the sacrifice of the holy Lamb of God, Jesus Christ.

After two days I was completely ready to lay my life in the arms of Jesus. A home meeting had been mentioned at the church, but I hadn't paid close attention to its location because I didn't think I would be interested. But after two days of reading the New Testament, everything had changed. I longed for full connection with Jesus, and I didn't want to wait an extra minute. As I walked down the street where I thought the meeting was, I prayed that the Lord would help me find the right door. There were lots of buildings and entrances on the street, but the first door I knocked on was the apartment where these believers were meeting. Without question, God's hand was leading me.

I needed to know what to do to receive this Jesus. I needed Christ – I understood that clearly – I just didn't know what I should do to get him into my life. I had heard many other voices, from childhood, telling me that Christianity was the worst religion, the most miserable way to live, and that all Christians were going to hell – but these all disappeared, and only one voice stood out for me. This persistent voice was the most beautiful, safe voice I had ever heard. It attracted me and called me in the depths of my being. I was ready to go to the end of the world to receive Christ into my life, although I did not understand much of the Bible.

At the home meeting, I learned what I needed to do: to repent and dedicate my life to him, which I did with great pleasure. My conversion was sincere, unwavering, uncompromising, and I immediately devoted myself to him without reserve and started seeking close relationship with the Lord with my whole heart. My conversion took place on 28 November 2000. I will never forget the heavenly joy that filled my being when I prayed the prayer of repentance and surrendered my life to Jesus. The believers all prayed for me. After that meeting, as I went back through the city to my home, I felt like I was flying. Unspeakable joy flowed through me. I wanted to sing, dance, and share my joy with the whole world.

From that moment my life turned in a completely new direction. Fasting, prayer and studying the Word soon became a way of life for me. Of course, when I read the Bible, there was a lot that I didn't understand right away, and so I connected with more mature Christians for help. Elena became my mentor. She was a wonderful example to imitate in the way she lived out the love and character of Christ. I will never forget what this sister did for me in that, often difficult, period of my life. I thank God for sending her to me.

Only now did I understand the meaning of that long-ago dream of God standing beside me and the real agony of knowing that I was separated from him. When I was yet a little girl, the Eternal God lovingly showed me how great he was and how far from him I was as a sinful human being. Now I knew that the only way to reach him was through the holy sacrifice of the spotless Lamb – Christ! This knowledge that he forgets no one and offers salvation to everyone, including me, warmed and strengthened my heart and filled me with great hope. I found the true Lord who himself is love. This was what I had been longing for, in all those years of loneliness and dark discouragement. His name is Jesus Christ – Isa Masikh – Jesus the Messiah.

My long-tormented quest for meaning in life had come to an end. Now a new quest began, but this new quest was joyful and full of hope, inspiration and purpose. This quest was for close fellowship with God. I was filled with an all-consuming hunger to know the Most High God intimately and to fulfil his will. (This will go forward, unceasingly, to the end of my days, and I love the process!)

Such a deep hunger and thirst awoke in me towards God that for a period of time, I largely forgot about my songs, my performances, my concerts. I just filled my life with reading God's holy Word, with fasting and prayer. All of those things that before had seemed so important, now retreated to a secondary plane. I was like a little child who for long years had been starving and, at last, was offered an abundance of delicious food. I was so thankful!

As I studied the Bible and other Christian literature, I began to get to know God in a completely new way. More and more I fell in love with my Creator God. He was not so far distant and silent as I had feared, but he loved me unconditionally with a kind, fatherly love. He forgave me and wanted close fellowship with me; he personally watched over and cared for me. This Father God was the one to whom I could totally entrust myself. I wanted to draw near to him and serve him with all of my being.

Before long I passionately desired the covenant step of water baptism, uniting with Jesus in his death and resurrection. To be baptized in someone's bath just didn't seem serious enough to me. I wanted to be baptized outdoors in the sea, no matter how hard it might be – even if it was December! The revelation I had received of the true God and his will for my life was so earth-shaking that I could not allow even the slightest hint of compromise in my response. As I think back, I smile at myself a little; but at that time I literally wanted to demonstrate to God how serious I was in my relationship with him and that he deserved the very best I had to give. I trembled to think of disappointing him and couldn't wait to enter into this full covenant with my Lord.

The weather was typical December winter. I needed a courageous Christian leader who would agree to plunge into the freezing waters of the Caspian Sea with me. After a few days, my mentor, Elena, told me she had found the heroic pastor who was ready to sacrifice himself. His name was Kamal.

I asked my youngest sister to help me prepare a festive meal for a grand event.

'I am preparing to celebrate the greatest event in my life,' I told her.

'What?' my sister exclaimed. 'Is Russia giving you the Honoured Performing Artist of the Republic Award?' That was the highest honour that could be accorded a musician in my country, and she could imagine nothing that would excite me more.

I smiled inside and said, 'A title like that is not even an "event" in comparison to what I am preparing to celebrate.'

My sister was visibly confused and could not grasp what could be so much more important to me than national honours, but she and a Muslim friend helped me to prepare the food at my apartment.

17 December 2000. On that morning when I planned to be baptized, I was a lump of pain from an inflammation. When I came to the meeting of believers, everything in my body hurt, and I could not even stand during the worship time. But I was not about to retreat from this most important event. With great difficulty I struggled to my feet at the end of the worship service and cried out to God for help.

At that moment Madina, whose testimony of transformation had brought me unknowingly to the church, came running with a booklet of spiritual inspiration. She began to pray for me. The Lord put in her mouth words of powerful encouragement that were exactly what I needed to hear. Subsequently, she became one of the most important people in my life – often used of God to bring me huge strength and encouragement at critical moments. How remarkable and marvellous are the ways of the Lord!

The weather was even colder that day than it had been; the sea raged and the beach was deserted. When Kamal and I first tried to enter the water, a wave knocked us off our feet. The water was so cold, it took my breath away. In my frozen condition I couldn't utter a word. With my eyes, I pleaded with Kamal to hurry and complete the rite. Suddenly a huge wave submerged me. Finally Kamal baptized me in the name of the Lord. Wow! It was an amazing baptism. I was thrilled.

When I emerged from the water my pain was completely gone. The first thing that my mentor, Elena, said to me was, 'Shaadia, God himself baptized you!' She was right. I had felt that – when I had presented myself totally to the Lord and been buried under that huge wave. The old Shaadia, with all her sins and cursed existence, was buried in the raging waters of the Caspian Sea. And the new Shaadia had been born anew into the kingdom of God, not for her own glory, but for the glory of God.

Jesus replied, 'Very truly I tell you, no one can see the kingdom of God unless they are born again . . . no one can enter the kingdom of God unless they are born of water and the Spirit.'

John 3:3–5

Shortly after my baptism, I was awakened in the night by the voice of the Lord. 'I will open before you many doors around the world,' he said. 'Don't be afraid of anything.' A few days later, the same thing happened again, word for word. Suddenly, I remembered hearing those exact words before – when I was so ill following my abortion. With great sadness I realized that if I had believed in Jesus earlier, so many painful things would not have happened, including that perhaps most painful of all.

I had never wanted to talk about the experience with anyone, not even myself. If it were possible to erase something from my history, this episode would be top of my list. When Jesus came into my life, he forgave me, healed me, and freed me from my past. As a result I am now able to speak peacefully about that terrible time and how Jesus is redeeming everything that happened to me for his purposes – even that.

And we know that in all things God works for the good of those who love him, who have been called according to his purpose.

Romans 8:28

Two and a half years had now passed since that tragic time. I came to know Jesus, my life had turned 180 degrees and, thank God, was moving in a totally new direction. But when I heard these words of promise twice from the Lord, and remembered how I had heard them in that earlier painful period, I realized how much God loved me. Even then, in the darkest moment of my life when, due to my sins, I deserved the just judgment of heaven, Jesus in his matchless love and mercy reached out to me. I survived those years only thanks to his amazing grace, faithfulness and love. I am eternally grateful to my Lord and pour out my heart of praise, honour and glory to him.

For I did not come to judge the world, but to save the world.

John 12:47

Over the intervening years, my relationship with Gadzhi, the father of my baby, had continued off and on. We saw each other much less frequently, partly due to his difficult circumstances; but for a couple of months after I came to Christ, although I only actually saw Gadzhi once, he was still in my life. It had not occurred to me to end our relationship. But, as I studied the Bible, it became clear to me that this relationship was displeasing to God. At first, I struggled to grasp this. What is so bad when two people love each other and get together physically? I was not selling myself. In Islam, a man is permitted to have four wives. Divorce and a new marriage is not a big problem.

But in the Bible this kind of non-covenant relationship is called 'immorality'. Human beings are so accustomed to sin and impurity, that life without those activities seems dull and boring to us. 'The heart is deceitful above all things and beyond cure' (Jeremiah 17:9), it says in the Word of God. But then in the next verse, these words of hope are heard, 'I the LORD search the heart.'

In the early period of my relationship with Jesus Christ, I struggled bluntly to acknowledge sin as sin and turn away from it. 'What am I supposed to do? Bury myself alive?' I wondered, but the reality was the complete opposite.

God – praise to him! – cleansed my mind and my heart and helped me to see things as he sees them. How horrible to live in impurity! What joy and awesome freedom to live in the light of Christ and in the peaceful holiness of the Lord!

Once I understood that I needed to end this unholy relationship with Gadzhi, I began to pray. I could not see how this could possibly happen. I remembered how, about a year earlier, I had decided to separate from him. Gadzhi went into a rage that I even dared to think about such a thing and came very close to killing me. He considered me his personal property, and felt that he was the only one who had a decision in this matter. With such a man as this, a woman does not leave; she stays or she dies. So now I knew only God could help me. I fervently prayed that God would separate this man from me. After a time of some fierce internal battle, I firmly decided to leave the relationship.

I asked everyone in my Christian home group to pray with me about my firm decision. From that moment, I literally never saw Gadzhi again. Over the next several months there were two short phone calls from him in the middle of the night, but then no more. Hard as it is to believe, he completely disappeared from my life. This was a genuine miracle and a testimony of God's faithfulness and power to me personally.

Once, one of my sisters, offended by my leaving Islam and embracing Jesus' way, verbally attacked Christians. She said that our church was mostly 'losers' – former drug addicts, broken people, fallen women. First of all, this wasn't actually true. People from a lot of different backgrounds were in our church. True enough, some came out of visibly sinful pasts, but for others, their past sins weren't outwardly visible at all. Many of these had become aware of their sinfulness only because of coming into contact with the shining light of Jesus. Secondly, this world is really unfair in the way it judges others. Out of pride, a person will often forget how sinful they themselves are. What does the Word of God say about this? 'All have sinned and fall short of the glory of God' (Romans 3:23).

Here's the beauty of God's love. The humble ones, who admit their sinfulness, through the grace of Jesus end up far ahead in well-being compared to the humanly proud ones. Isn't this wonderful?

God chose the foolish things of the world to shame the wise; God chose the weak things of the world to shame the strong. God chose the lowly things of this world and the despised things – and the things that are not – to nullify the things that are, so that no one may boast before him. It is because of him that you are in Christ Jesus, who has become for us wisdom from God – that is, our righteousness, holiness and redemption. Therefore, as it is written: 'Let the one who boasts boast in the Lord.'

1 Corinthians 1:27–31

A Muslim story tells how a woman caught in adultery was brought to Mohammed for judgment. He sent her away until the baby had been born, and then again until the baby had been weaned. Then and only then did he have her executed. When a similar woman was brought to Jesus in John 8, Jesus said, 'Let any one of you who is without sin be the first to throw a stone at her.' One by one her accusers left because none was without sin. 'Go now and leave your life of sin', Jesus told her.

Religion judges harshly, knows no mercy, and pushes a person towards death. But the true God offers to us a way of escape from the bondage of sin and gives salvation through the sacrifice of Jesus Christ. The true God offers this to us because he is love (see 1 John 4:8).

That woman in both stories is me. I know how Mohammed would have dealt with me. And I know how Jesus, full of grace and truth, responded to me. I made my choice.

The Word became flesh and made his dwelling among us . . . full of grace and truth . . . For the law was given through Moses; grace and truth came through Jesus Christ.

John 1:14,17

Grace – the Lord receives you just as you are, with all your inadequacies and faults, without reproach or judgment. Truth – he teaches you how to live and function properly. Grace comes with love and forgiveness and gives a person the desire and strength to actually change. Then truth lays out the direction and instructs you how to live this new life. Grace brings healing; truth brings direction – only Jesus brought this fully to our earth.

Many times I knelt in my room, seeking the Lord in prayer and worship, hungering and thirsting for his presence with all my being. His grace had powerfully changed my life, and I wanted all of him that I could possibly receive. On one of those days I read in the New Testament about the baptism of Jesus, and how the Holy Spirit had rested upon him in the form of a dove. I longed for the Lord to send the Holy Spirit to me also in the form of a dove.

One night I dreamed that a white dove flew into my room and circled the bright light on the ceiling above my bed. I awoke with a sense of ecstatic joy from this dream. Later that day, kneeling in prayer in my room, I raised my head. There sat the dove of my dream on the edge of the open upper window. He was looking at me.

I gasped from astonishment. After a few seconds I burst into new-found praise to my Lord with an overflowing heart! For three days this dove was my constant companion. He flew into the same spot each morning and sat looking at me throughout the day as if he were my closest friend. I never saw a white dove near my window or on my balcony before or after that time, but from that day I knew the Holy Spirit was active and powerfully working in my life.

That year I was a new-born babe in Christ. I am very thankful to God for this special encouragement regarding the presence of the Holy Spirit. From that time on, the Holy Spirit became my closest, most present, Friend.

5

The Cost of True Love

For a person growing up Muslim to become a Christian is not a small step. Such a person pays a high price. Most of the time it will cost everything, and maybe even life itself. A person making this decision inevitably faces a choice between everything they have known in this world and the love of Jesus Christ. The Islamic faith is not tolerant towards those who leave Islam. This is considered the greatest possible shame and disgrace for an Islamic family. Usually the entire clan of the converted person shares the same sense of deep disgrace. In most cases persecution comes, not only from the relatives but also from the highest clan leadership.

Many new converts are unable to hold out against the extreme pressure to return to Islam – verbal scorn, threats, violence, malicious insults, beatings, torture and every conceivable harassment. Sometimes things are done that you can't even call 'beastliness' because, honestly, beasts are not capable of the depths of cruelty that a deceived human being can conjure up and commit against another. Blindness seems to accompany the depths of religious zealotry. Many who have turned away from Islam and come to Christ have paid with their very lives.

Soon after breaking off my relationship with Gadzhi and the breakthrough of the Holy Spirit in my life, I prepared to travel to our mountain region to visit my parents. Our home village was about three hours by car from Temer-Kala, the regional capital where I lived. About once a month I travelled to the mountains and did whatever I could to help my parents. On this occasion I had prepared my bags, ready to depart the next morning. That night I sensed a strong spiritual unease, something restraining me from this trip as if protecting me from some great unknown danger. I didn't understand it at all, but experienced an intense spirit of prayer. All I desired was to pray without ceasing. Every cell of my being seemed to groan and cry out to God. And in all this, I hardly uttered a word.

Of course, in this condition I didn't travel anywhere. I remained in a continual state of prayer for nearly two weeks. Then in the third week, the fervent intercession subsided, and my heart was filled with peace. About a week after that I travelled to see my parents in the mountains.

The year was 2001. There were no cell phone connections at that point. When I arrived at my parents' home, the first thing my mother said when she saw me was, 'How glad I am that you didn't come earlier! I was so afraid! Your father was waiting for you, resolved to burying you alive because of your faith in Christ!'

My mother described it all. Several influential men in my home village had come to my father and convinced him of the horrible shame brought on the family by his daughter betraying the faith of the ancestors and turning to Christianity. People knew I had become a Christian because I was famous in my republic, and had not been quiet in sharing Jesus with my friends. Christians had also started 'preaching' that Shaadia Firoz was in their church! Only in killing me could he cleanse the family line from this terrible disgrace. When I heard this, I dissolved in wholehearted praise to God for his faithfulness and protection. I rejoiced in the truth of his Word, which is living and active in us in the power of the Holy Spirit. For his Word says:

> In the same way, the Spirit helps us in our weakness. We do not know what we ought to pray for, but the Spirit himself intercedes for us through wordless groans.
>
> Romans 8:26

Our precious Holy Spirit knew how to intercede in exactly the right way for me and for my father. He rescued me from deadly danger, and rescued my father from committing murder.

When I did arrive in the village after my two weeks of intense prayer, my father was in an unusually peaceful state and didn't say one negative word to me, but the evening of the next day, he suddenly fell seriously ill. His temperature shot up to 40 degrees Celsius (104 degrees Fahrenheit), and he became delirious. My mother panicked. In all her life, she'd never seen him like this, and probably this was the end. The doctor rushed to us and diagnosed my father with advanced double pneumonia. We had to get him to the regional hospital immediately, but with his weak heart and high fever, to transport him twenty-five kilometres over rough mountain roads would have been the same as killing him.

I shut myself up in my room and began praying fervently and passionately to the Lord for mercy for my father and healing for his body. When I came out, I was astonished to discover that my father only wanted to receive personal care from me. If I moved from his side, he began to search for me with his eyes; he only became peaceful again when I sat beside him. Miraculously, about two hours after my intercessory prayer in my room, his fever completely dissipated, and there were no indicators of any sickness in his lungs. The next morning he was completely healthy! After this, God gave me favour for a while to tell my father about Jesus; I was even able to lay my hands on him and pray for him.

My mother had grown up in a small mountain village where they had a strong reverence and honour for Isa Masikh (Jesus the Messiah) in their religious practices. As a result, she more openly and peacefully responded to my faith in Jesus Christ from the beginning. Almost immediately she noticed the positive changes that had come into my life after my conversion. Although on the outside I was a good daughter, providing for my parents and visiting regularly, only after I met Jesus did I realize how evil I was on the inside; how much pain and poison was in my heart. I was often rude, stubborn, dominating and rebellious towards my mother. I repented before my parents for not being a good daughter at all, and for my wickedness and lies. My mother also noted how God answered my prayers. Mama herself had always responded to God with deep reverence and tenderness. I thank God for her. She had no earthly inheritance to bequeath to me and hardly any words of teaching about life, but the main thing – the most precious thing – which she gave, was her heart for the true God. Her kindness, honesty, and her reverence for the Creator spoke more loudly than any words.

During these same weeks I experienced an amazing, vivid vision. It wasn't a dream, and it wasn't an actual physical event. It was something of a different nature – a revelation that was distinct, clear, real and yet not something that you can tangibly categorize. In this vision a huge Bible descended into my outstretched hands. In the next moment I could see the whole world through the open Bible. Golden letters remained visible while the rest of the book was entirely translucent. The world was covered in darkness and gloom, but from the holy words flowed a quiet, gentle light. This vision filled my heart with confidence and peace. In some mysterious way, it was made clear that God was calling me to carry his Word to people, to teach and to preach. I was overcome with fear.

I had always had an overwhelming fear of speaking in front of people. In the culture where I grew up, people are stingy with compliments and praise. They fear putting a jinx on anyone; as a result, words of encouragement were extremely rare, and criticism, abundant. Judgment and negativity were so omnipresent that if (rarely) someone stood up for me and spoke a positive word, I would most likely begin to sob. People close to me so frequently told me that I was stupid and brainless that subconsciously I started seeing myself that way – and many times acted that way. After I became a famous singer, giving an interview or speaking at a public event was sheer torture. I always avoided speaking obligations if I possibly could. If I absolutely couldn't dodge it, I prepared the shortest possible speech and memorized it in advance word for word, so that, hopefully, I wouldn't embarrass myself.

Just a few days after that vivid revelation with the huge Bible, a Christian sister with an intercessory ministry told me she had had a prophetic dream. I was called to carry the Word of God to people, to teach and to preach in an extensive ministry, she said. A few months later I had the opportunity to travel to America. In a number of churches there, while people were praying for me, more than one gave a prophetic word about God calling me to teach and preach his Word. The following year, I had the unexpected joy of travelling to Israel. There, during a time of prayer in a Christian gathering, an older leader prophesied the exact same thing about God's calling on my life.

As these confirmations continued to come, I gradually started to believe that the Lord really was calling me. In response, I earnestly prayed that he would give me the needed opportunities to study his Word and receive spiritual training. In my local church in Temer-Kala, I completed every training school and Bible study course which the church offered. I practically devoured any quality Christian books, tapes or videos that crossed my path. I eagerly attended training conferences held at other locations and thirsted for God's wisdom more than anything. It was a great adventure of throwing myself into knowing the Lord, listening to his voice, and taking small steps to fulfil this new-found calling. In the process, I undoubtedly made many mistakes. There is a saying that goes something like this: 'The only one who makes no mistakes, is the one who does nothing at all.' Quite often I was comforted with that thought.

The insane idea that killing an unfaithful one or an apostate guarantees heaven has driven some deceived Muslims to murder innocent people – who have only exercised their freedom of will in making a spiritual decision. These deceived ones don't understand that they are daring to function as judges and executioners, placing themselves higher than God himself. In blindness they don't realize that they are being propelled into this evil by none other than Satan. What a horrible deception! Forgive them, Lord, 'for they do not know what they are doing' (see Luke 23:34).

Thank God, many dear ones are not like this. Among the people of my birth culture, there are many wise, God-fearing people, seeking after truth. With such it is possible to peacefully discuss and consider important spiritual questions. But, unfortunately, just as one spoonful of tar can ruin a whole barrel of honey, so also just one destructive person can instigate a huge amount of devastation.

From the beginning of my new life in Jesus, I understood all of this perfectly clearly. Many times, from childhood on, I had heard horrible violent stories about people being killed who had dared to turn away from Islam. But I had made my choice and was prepared to pay the cost. Indeed, there was no price that could remotely compare to the joy of life in Jesus. What I gained was incomparably greater than anything I could possibly lose (see Philippians 3:7,8). I firmly decided to hold on tightly to Jesus, no matter what. I knew that all would be well because no one or nothing could separate me from his love (see Romans 8:38,39).

To say that I was not fearful at all would not be correct; there were times when reality was very frightening. More than once I experienced real shuddering in my heart as I took my first timid, but determined, steps in my new faith. My situation was intensified due to my fame in my home region, which was more fiercely Muslim than ever now that communism was past. Furthermore, early on, some of the folk from the House of Prayer spread the news about my conversion, perhaps too rapidly – before I had time to become spiritually strengthened and prepared for the onslaught.

People say, 'You find out who your true friends are when you go through a difficult time.' It's true. I found out how many true friends I had. But, beyond that, I had the benefit of many new brothers and sisters in a big new family of God. This was a huge comfort, strength, and encouragement to me.

I received serious threats, sometimes from people I knew and sometimes from people I had never met. Occasionally these threats came to me by telephone in threatening voices. They scared me by saying that they would ban my music. They said

I would lose everything I had worked so hard to attain. They shouted that if I dared to appear on stage again, I would be stoned by people in the crowd. Former friends said I had gone out of my mind; they made fun of me. They acted as if I was in some kind of cult. All sorts of evil slander circulated regarding me, along with unbelievably absurd rumours. More than once I was threatened with death.

God refined me like silver through these tribulations, and I undoubtedly matured spiritually at a quicker pace. I had to. The more intense the difficulties, the more passionately I dug into the Word of God, prayed and fasted. My faith grew. I fell more and more deeply in love with my amazing Lord, and he comforted me with his incomparable presence and gave me joy through the indwelling power of his Holy Spirit.

Due either to fear or to religious antagonism, my large circle of friends and supporters abandoned me one by one. Only two or three in that once-large circle proved to be true friends.

One of these was Makhmood Kurbanovich, an amazing friend and gentleman. I think of him with deep warmth in my heart. This honourable person – a real gentleman – was one of those rare men with whom I could enjoy genuine friendship without any fear. Makhmood treated me like a real person, worthy of respect and honour, a woman, not some female morsel to drag into bed. He was a man of high position with great authority in society, and he honoured me by publicly displaying our genuine friendship, even after my conversion to Christ. I am extremely thankful to Makhmood for his character, his quality, and his kindness. In a society where men constantly displayed their immoral conquests of women, this man gifted me with pure unconditional friendship. He rose above narrow religious prejudices and continued our warm friendship even when many in society had turned against me. In this, he risked his own reputation, and I honour him and am thankful to him for this.

And I cannot be silent about Nurjan – my dear female friend and an amazing person. We got to know each other in 1995 when Nurjan captured my heart with her forceful character, her honesty, and generosity of spirit. Not only this, but also her generosity, and her capability to genuinely love. Almost immediately we became close friends, and I also developed a real closeness with her family. In those years she was the finest person God sent into my life. When I told her of my conversion to Christ, she was initially upset, but she didn't turn away from our friendship even though news of my new faith spread far and wide, and many rejected me with contempt as an apostate.

During this same year, Nurjan's mother became very ill. I sensed the Holy Spirit leading me to visit her and take the *Jesus* film in her native language. I was afraid at first, but not wanting to be disobedient to the Lord, I visited her. We watched the *Jesus* film together. She watched peacefully, and we were able to talk about it. The film seemed to touch her deeply, but she showed no particular enthusiasm. I prayed fervently and fasted for her and for all of Nurjan's family, but our relationship was no longer as close as it had once been. Later I learned that just before her death, Nurjan's mother requested Nurjan never turn away from her friendship with me, no matter what other people said. I was very touched by this. I do not know what moved her to give this kind of direction to her daughter before her death. Maybe I will find out in heaven.

I was under a lot of pressure in those days, and the friendship of these few who continued in warm relationship meant a lot to me. I continue to pray for them, with hope and faith that they will respond to the call of God. I love my friends very much, including also those who judged and rejected me. My burning desire is that they would take hold of the life-changing grace of Jesus, as I did.

> I have told you these things, so that in me you may have peace. In this world you will have trouble. But take heart! I have overcome the world.
>
> John 16:33

I loved my oldest sister very much. She was hard-working, determined and talented in so many ways. She graduated from high school with honours, but just before her entrance exams for university she had an attack of appendicitis. She was rushed to the hospital for emergency surgery, but it did not go well. Medical complications followed. She endured many months lying in the hospital, and her university enrolment was delayed for a year. In a tragic combination of events, the next summer right before her entrance exams, she suffered a terrible car accident. This accident caused major spinal injuries, and she became bedridden. According to the doctors, there was no chance of her ever regaining mobility.

In our family circle there was no one able to give her the care she needed. It wasn't in my father's character – at least outwardly – to show compassion to any of his children when they were suffering. He didn't consider it necessary to take any significant measures on behalf of my sister. My dear mama, under the autocratic control of my father, felt unable to do anything either.

From childhood I felt that my father utterly loathed weakness or illness in any form. He, himself, as he explained, simply overcame illness by the power of his will. In my younger years, if he ever found me in bed with a high fever, would kick me out physically and force me to school or to the field for work.

He had no patience for any type of weakness but immediately labelled it 'laziness'. Many times I remember sitting at school with my head bursting from painful ear infections, but I kept going, regardless of physical suffering.

In the early days, still under the Soviets, our available medical help was besmirched with bribery, corruption and extreme partiality. To get full medical treatment you had to either bribe a doctor or gain access through a powerful person. Neither of those options was available for my sister. But, thanks to the strength of her will and constant physical exercise, she actually got back on her feet to some extent and was able to do some light work, although officially she was always disabled. University was no longer an option.

Due to our mother's extreme busyness and exhaustion working long hours on the collective farm, this sister, as the eldest daughter, had taken on a huge load of household responsibilities from a young age. She was robbed of childhood playtime and joys. Frequently she bore the brunt of our father's drunken, degrading and abusive behaviours. Fears, endless labour, insults and tears filled my sister's life. All this, combined with her tragic health problems, took a toll on her spirit and outlook on life. Following the unsuccessful operation and the car accident, she became tight-lipped, impatient and almost cruel – even though she had been a different person previously.

Her deeply wounded soul, burdened with all of this overwhelming trauma and pain, hid its beauty under a protective shell with a thorny exterior. She began to seek comfort in various forms of mysticism and occult spirituality. She hadn't been particularly religious before. Although she considered herself Muslim, she had never been active in Islamic worship or rituals. Horoscopes, palm reading, acupuncture, fortune telling and magic practices interested her far more.

I was sorry that my sister had suffered so grievously from this accident and with so many health difficulties. For years I tried to do everything I could to help, as her younger sister. When I came to know Jesus, with great joy and hope, I hurried to see her and tell her that the loving Jesus could heal her completely. I naively thought she would rejoice in this possibility. But after I told her what Jesus had done for me, she started hearing voices that told her that I was extremely dangerous, that I wanted to kill her and all of the family. My sister believed these unholy voices straight from the pit of hell and totally rejected me.

Many in this world severely underestimate the power and reality of the spiritual world in which a constant battle is underway for the souls of human beings. Nothing and no one strikes fear into Satan like the name of Jesus. He will go to the most extreme lengths and use the most deceptive tactics to keep you from faith in Jesus.

> And even if our gospel is veiled, it is veiled to those who are perishing. The god of this age has blinded the minds of unbelievers, so that they cannot see the light of the gospel that displays the glory of Christ, who is the image of God.
>
> 2 Corinthians 4:3,4

> Your father, the devil . . . was a murderer from the beginning, not holding to the truth, for there is no truth in him. When he lies, he speaks his native language, for he is a liar and the father of lies.
>
> John 8:44

It was unbearable to see my sister suffer. Day and night I cried out to my heavenly Father in fasting and prayer for her, but she became more and more fierce in her hatred. She didn't want to see or hear me. For a long time I looked for a way to connect with her, knowing full well what was going on and longing to be able to help her.

Finally, the voices and visions so tormented her that she decided to go to a psychiatric hospital. After the psychiatric hospital, she turned strongly towards Islam. The hospital and Islam did not diminish her hatred towards me or towards Jesus; on the contrary, it intensified. For many years I have lived with the continual hope of healing and deliverance for my sister, but she firmly believes that I am a dangerous person and a threat to her and our entire family. She won't tolerate my presence around her. On a rare occasion when we end up in the same location and I seek to speak a word with her, she simply ignores me.

Once, when I was home from college on holiday, we met at my brother's house. I hadn't seen her for two years. I tried to converse with her, but she literally twisted away from me. She muttered something in my direction in a hateful tone. I couldn't restrain myself. I ran from the room, gasping with tears and anguish. I told God that it was hopeless and useless to do anything. 'I pray for her so much; nothing ever changes!'

At that moment, vividly within myself, I heard these two verses from God's Word: 'If you forgive anyone's sins, their sins are forgiven; if you do not forgive them, they are not forgiven' (John 20:23) and 'Above all, love each other deeply, because love covers over a multitude of sins' (1 Peter 4:8).

These verses opened in my spirit with new depth and meaning that I had never seen before. Peace and rest filled my heart. I understood that while I forgive, pray and cover my sister with the love of God, the chance remains open for her salvation. 'Lord, as long as I live, I will forgive, pray for, and love my sister,' I exclaimed aloud with joy and trust in the Lord. 'And with this I will always be full of hope, because you are true to your Word!'

I hungered for change in my sister, but God hungered to see change in me. Was I ready to love her just as she is, even if I never saw change in her? Could I patiently, lovingly and unconditionally honour who she was as a person and her freedom of choice as a human being? It's love that would work miracles – first of all changing my own heart and soul.

I am still not able to have an active relationship with my sister, but I continue praying for her and loving her. I will not give up hope that one day she will open her heart to the one who is love, to the one who is the only Saviour. On that day she will experience his delightful love and warm touch, full of compassion and goodness. This grace of Jesus is the single thing capable of freeing, healing, cleansing and changing a human life from the inside, but the person must first desire this and be open to it. God never forces anyone. He offers free choice. Jesus knocks at the door of each person's life.

The devil, on the other hand, is a murderer who rudely and aggressively asserts his power. No one who serves the true God and Jesus Christ, sent by him, and who is led by the Holy Spirit, can hate or kill another person. But the Murderer leads people into all kinds of deception and error. He instils hate, murder and endless ugly behaviours in the human race.

In the end, each person chooses whom they will side with – both for this life and for eternity. As long as I live, I will not stop praying for my family and my dear friends – those who presently reject their own salvation, not knowing what they are doing.

> Here I am! I stand at the door and knock. If anyone hears my voice and opens the door, I will come in and eat with that person, and they with me.
>
> Revelation 3:20

6

A New Love Song

Coming to a place of trusting God in everything and being at peace in his will was a huge process for me. For so many years I had done everything on my own, and had learned to think that way. At the time I came to Christ, I was in the midst of preparing for an upcoming solo concert. Now that I was in relationship with Jesus, I wondered what to do. Should I continue giving big concerts like before? By this time I had received serious threats that if I went onto the stage again, they would stone me and kill me right there. So I started praying to seek the Lord's leading. After several days of prayer and fasting, the Lord spoke to me. 'Go ahead; don't fear anything. I will be with you, and you will see my glory.'

Total peace filled my heart with this clarity. Whatever difficulties and threats came my way didn't hold power over me any more. The bottom line is this: The words of people or the difficulty of circumstances are nothing in comparison to the clear direction of Almighty God. The apostle John says in the Bible, 'You, dear children, are from God and have overcome them, because the one who is in you is greater than the one who is in the world' (1 John 4:4). When a person trusts and surrenders to the goodness of God, that is when miracles happen. That is when the light of God shines brilliantly through that life.

I gave myself into God's hands.

The concert took place on 21 March 2001. Advance tickets were sold out a number of days ahead. A crowd stood outside the auditorium, unable to get tickets. I had invited all my believer friends to be present at this concert. The whole church fellowship was praying in agreement, specifically for God's blessing on every listener. I even enlisted strong Christian men to supervise the concert hall. I had one burning desire within my soul, that my concert would be a wonderful gift to each person attending or watching on TV, and my heart was full of God's love for them.

I did not sing specifically spiritual songs and did not say one religious word about Jesus. I didn't want to look pious or engage in something overtly 'religious'. I dressed in the typical national costume which I usually dressed in for my concerts. The only difference in this concert was inside me. My life now was totally surrendered to the Most High God, and Jesus Christ, in his grace and glory, had full reign within me. Other than that, this was a typical secular concert – like all my previous concerts. But the Almighty God was there with unspeakable joy.

Before dawn the next morning my phone began ringing. My fans had always been a source of great joy to me, and I reciprocated with genuine expressions of my delight in them and how I loved them. This time, quite a few people told me that during this concert they had been healed. For some it was emotional healing. For others direct physical healing had taken place. A huge encouragement and confirmation to me was when a medical doctor, an acquaintance of mine, described how he had received a supernatural healing in his body during my concert. This, of course, was the result of the presence of the glory of God.

Of all the concerts I took part in, this concert was far beyond anything else. Others told me it was the greatest concert they had ever seen in our region of the northern Caucasus. Following this concert I was presented with the highest artistic award, Honoured Performing Artist of the Republic. I return all glory, honour and praise to my Lord for this concert and the award.

That night I discovered for myself that our Creator is not a religious God. He hates false religiosity, but he loves *people* with a perfect and unconditional love. He longs for each person to live life to the full according to his Word. To please God and to fully respond to him is possible only by faith.

> Without faith it is impossible to please God, because anyone who comes to him must believe that he exists and that he rewards those who earnestly seek him.
>
> Hebrews 11:6

The downfall of human beings is not the lack of attention to certain religious practices and norms; the downfall is the infection of sin in each person. And the root of sin is in the human heart. There's not much benefit in all our efforts to clean the outside of the cup when the inside of the cup remains full of dirt. In exactly the same way, there's not much benefit in observing religious norms if the inner heart of the person remains unchanged. Jesus severely rebuked the hypocrisy of religious people in his time.

> Woe to you, teachers of the law and Pharisees, you hypocrites! You clean the outside of the cup and dish, but inside they are full of greed and self-indulgence. Blind Pharisee! First clean the inside of the cup and dish, and then the outside also will be clean. Woe to you, teachers of the law and Pharisees, you hypocrites! You are like whitewashed tombs, which look beautiful on the outside but on the inside are full of the bones of the dead and everything unclean.

In the same way, on the outside you appear to people as righteous
but on the inside you are full of hypocrisy and wickedness.

Matthew 23:25–28

Only the blood of Jesus Christ has the power to cleanse the
human heart. Only his love has the capacity to change a human
life from the inside out.

My beloved aunt was upset about my turning to faith in
Jesus the Messiah. 'Islam is the cleanest, purest religion,' she
said. 'A true Muslim completes a washing, cleansing process
five times a day, but Christians don't do that.'

I responded, 'To observe ritual washing is a fine thing, and
anyone can do that, but tell me, dear aunt, how can a person wash and cleanse his heart? Look around at how much
offence, judgment, pain and unforgiveness exist in the hearts
of so many people. Sin is lodged deep inside us. Only Jesus offers the means of cleansing our hearts from sin – his own holy
blood.' My dear aunt could find no words to respond.

A few months after this concert I decided to schedule another. The decision was based on the pressure of people around
me. I didn't seek the Lord's will and wisdom. Ticket sales wer-
en't great. Everything seemed to be working against me.

The concert itself went well, by the grace of God, but –
sitting in the dressing room – I felt empty and unsatisfied
inside. I asked God what he wanted to say to me through all
of this. It was at that moment that the Lord spoke to my heart.
'Shaadia, I want you to leave everything and follow me. What
you have seen to this point is nothing in comparison to what I
want to do in your life.'

That night I realized God wanted 100 per cent of my life.
He was not interested in halfway measures or halfway relationships or compromises.

I passionately wanted to follow the Lord, nonetheless, at the beginning it was difficult for me to understand why I should leave everything that I had worked so hard for. After all, I could earn lots of money to give to God's work. And, the bottom line, how would I live if I gave up my singing career? It was the only way I knew to earn an income.

'My dear heavenly Father, have I come to you only to lose everything? I thought it was supposed to be the opposite. Don't you love me? Now, if I continued this career together with you, I could earn lots of money to use for your kingdom.' Those were the kinds of words I poured out to God.

'For my thoughts are not your thoughts,
   neither are your ways my ways,'
   declares the LORD.
'As the heavens are higher than the earth,
   so are my ways higher than your ways
   and my thoughts than your thoughts.'

Isaiah 55:8,9

I had to learn that God's standards are not human standards, and that his love is far beyond our understanding of love. God does not need my money; he already possesses endless resources. What he desires is my life. He wants to transform my character. He wanted to reorientate my entire worldview and give me new foundations of life and well-being. I needed to learn to rest in him and totally trust him.

God set before me a choice. I made that choice, deciding to totally trust him with everything. Even though there was much I still did not understand, I said 'Yes' to his plan for my life and 'No' to my personal ambitions. I cancelled my remaining concerts and did not take any more engagements.

In the end, I left everything behind. The rest of my friends turned away from me. My father was so enraged – both about my cancelling the concerts and becoming a Christian – that he wanted to kill me. My acquaintances and relatives began to deal with me contemptuously. I was at the peak of my career, but I turned away from all of it and embraced faith in Jesus Christ. They could imagine nothing worse. I suffered to see my closest friends and family go through this turmoil and reject me. But most painful was to see them reject the truth and the Source that could give them peace, well-being and salvation.

Sometimes I would meet someone from my former close circle of friends on the street. 'Oh, are you still alive?' they would say – to which I would answer that never had I been more alive.

On several occasions influential people came to me and told me that if I returned to Islam, having given Christianity a quick try, many things would fall in my lap, things that I could hardly dream of. I could have the world on a silver platter, and my life would take on fairy tale dimensions of glamour and prestige. These people were aggressive, and warned me that if I went the other way, they could guarantee a horrible fate.

The devil offered Jesus a similar chance to choose the world's wisdom instead of God's.

The devil led him up to a high place and showed him in an instant all the kingdoms of the world. And he said to him, 'I will give you all their authority and splendour; it has been given to me, and I can give it to anyone I want to. If you worship me, it will all be yours.' Jesus answered, 'It is written: "Worship the Lord your God and serve him only."'

Luke 4:5–8

Praise be to our mighty God that Jesus rejected this temptation offered to him by Satan. Instead he obediently chose a shameful death on the cross to fulfil the will of his heavenly Father and free all of humanity from the slavery of sin! Satan, the father of lies, employs the same tactics today. He attempts to seduce us by using people and situations to drag us away from God and his purposes for our lives.

Not only will I never agree to a similar seductive offer, but I am prepared in addition to give away everything again if it might lead to winning one more person to Jesus' grace and redemption. I grieve at the – not just sad – but truly horrible eternal future that awaits those who reject Jesus Christ and his sacrificial death for their sins.

I decided to no longer worry about my reputation in the eyes of this transient world, and instead, seek my joy in Jesus' heavenly kingdom with all my heart.

Heartfelt thanks to our great patriarch Moses, who set a tremendous example for us. In the New Testament it says this about him: 'He chose to be ill-treated along with the people of God rather than to enjoy the fleeting pleasures of sin. He regarded disgrace for the sake of Christ as of greater value than the treasures of Egypt, because he was looking ahead to his reward' (Hebrews 11:25–26).

The process of my growth in faith was not easy or without pain and struggle. I thank God for wonderful, mature Christians whom he sent into my life at just the right time. They greatly helped me to become spiritually established and understand the real living Christ.

At this time a close sister in the Lord and I ended up in Moscow to attend a seminar focused on Christian growth. During that week she suggested that we visit her friends, Philip and Alice, who were temporarily in Moscow. It was a cold day in the middle of the winter. When Philip met us at the Metro, he immediately made a powerful impression on me – a tall, thin man in his middle years, simply and lightly dressed, including humble, functional shoes. Nothing was typical for freezing Moscow weather. Amazing humility, gentleness, peaceful confidence and holy divine love flowed out of him. Although we were meeting for the first time, it seemed as if I had known him for years.

Fellowship with this couple was like a healing balm to my heart. I felt like I had met with Jesus, who lives within humble, real people. Meeting such genuine servants of God during that intensely difficult period could not have been accidental. In the life yielded to the Lord, I concluded, there is no such thing as coincidence. Rather, in the life open to him, the Lord works like a Master Painter applying the exact strokes of his brush in just the right way on to the canvas of our life.

> For the eyes of the LORD range throughout the earth to strengthen those whose hearts are fully committed to him.
>
> 2 Chronicles 16:9

This new relationship served as a powerful encouragement and impetus in my spiritual growth. I left their place that evening a different person. I was filled with joy, hope and a readiness to serve the Most High with all my being. Fellowship times with these blessed friends continues to bring me personal encouragement and strengthens my faith. I value their wise counsel, which more than once has been God's provision for me during an intense period of growth.

Part Three

More of Jesus

Now the Lord is the Spirit; and where the Spirit of the Lord is, there is freedom.
And we all, who with unveiled faces reflect the Lord's glory, are being transformed into his image with ever-increasing glory, which comes from the Lord, who is the Spirit.

2 Corinthians 3:17,18

7

Growing Love

So, the first big trial of my faith was the decision to leave my singing career. This was particularly difficult because, as I have said, I was at the peak of my career. I had invested a huge amount of effort in it, and humanly speaking, singing was what I loved to do more than anything. But God, out of his incomprehensible love, had even more for me. This was only the beginning. Soon after this decision, the next major step of faith in my life commenced – a journey to South Africa.

From the very beginning of my new life in Jesus, the dream had burned in my heart to study in a Bible college in preparation for serving the Lord. A school in Moscow would have been more accessible to me. It was not so terribly far from my home region, and the arrangements and study would have been in Russian, a language with which I was now comfortable – my native language being Avar. But I was no longer lord of my own life; I had a Lord who was incomparably wiser and who loved me very much. He knew in all things what would be best for me. So I began to pray and fast, like never before, for God's wisdom and direction in this decision.

I had become acquainted with the pastors and leaders of Word of Life Church in Moscow and had been invited to study at their Bible college. I made preparations and was ready to fly to Moscow the following day. My suitcase was already packed, but on that last evening the Lord spoke clearly to my heart. I was not to go to Moscow; God was sending me to study in South Africa. I unpacked my suitcase and began to prepare for a much longer journey.

I had learned about CREARE International Bible School of the Arts from some girls who had attended a short-term training programme sponsored by them in Russia. I had dreamed of a school with a musical, artistic specialization, but didn't know there was such a thing. Even when I found this school, it seemed too difficult for me to be there. But when I made contact with the administration, they sent me an invitation to study, fulfilling my long-time dream.

But there was still the question of funds. Tuition and living expenses require a lot of money. Most of the money I had received from my last concert had been spent on a land purchase for a future local church and in gifts to servants of God in church ministry. What remained was a small reserve. Some acquaintances owed me a considerable sum of money that they promised to repay that month.

I utilized my reserve to make final preparations for the journey. By the time I had acquired the necessary visa and the plane tickets, only $100 (then approximately £57) remained in my pocket – all I possessed in the world. My English language skills were extremely weak, and I did not know anyone personally in South Africa. Besides, my parents were elderly. I didn't even know how long I would be gone. What if something major happened to them, and I was so far away I couldn't come back? Maybe I would never see them again. My heart tightened just thinking about this. Equally difficult was the prospect of leaving my young nephew. His mother, my youngest sister who had accompanied me to church on that first visit and helped me prepare the feast for my baptism, now lived in Turkey and rarely came back to our region. So the boy grew up with us, as close to me as if he had been my own son. The thought of leaving him was almost unbearable.

My plane ticket was one-way; beyond that I had just $100. But the Lord had made it clear that I was to go. In the final analysis, that was the key thing. He sees much further ahead than I ever could, and his wisdom is far beyond mine.

I am unbelievably grateful to God for the amazing support and understanding that I received from my own mother during this time. She was a huge encouragement, comfort and inspiration to my faith. From the beginning she strongly believed that God had a big plan for my life.

That did not mean things weren't difficult for her. She became extremely anxious and upset about my plans. It was beyond difficult for her to reconcile herself to the fact that I was going so terribly far away, and without anything.

I visited my parents' home for the last time just days before my departure for South Africa. That evening my mother and I shared our feelings about my upcoming journey, and expressed our fears and worries to each other. Throughout our conversation I tried to reassure her that everything would be fine, but I myself was experiencing a lot of stress. I had never before taken a step like this. In this atmosphere of considerable emotion, I fell asleep and dreamed.

In my dream I found myself in an unusual place full of total peace and bliss like I had never known before. There was a complete absence of any sense of time, or any framework related to time. Eternity. A Being approached me whom I somehow knew to be the Eternal One. He pressed me to his chest like I was a little girl. With deep sadness he said, 'Shaadia, I have done everything for you – why are you so worried?'

I was immediately ashamed of the anxiety I had been experiencing. I could see the total stupidity and groundlessness of any of my fears. So safe did I feel with him, so peaceful and good, that I was amazed that I had ever been able to worry about anything. 'He is so good,' I thought. 'We humans were created in his image and intended to resemble him, but we were corrupted. Lord, I so much want to look like you; and if I ever get married I hope with all my heart that my husband will live in your image and resemble you as much as possible.'

Then I awoke. In the morning I described my dream to my mother. This dream was a source of great joy to her.

That day as I travelled back to the city, the more I thought about the dream, the more filled with joy I became. My heavenly Father had already done everything; he was looking after everything on my behalf. God is so kind! He understood how difficult things had felt for me, and in his great wisdom and goodness personally gave me a gift, which would serve as a strong anchor for me. This was exactly what I needed; and this anchor would also strengthen me for future trials and difficulties in the journey ahead.

Many times my mother served as a bright ray of light in the midst of the darkest hours for me. May the Lord bless her abundantly and watch over her in Jesus' name.

I am a stranger on earth; do not hide your commands from me.
Psalm 119:19

On 8 January 2004 I sat inside the plane, still at the airport in Temer-Kala. In a few minutes the plane would lift off into the clouds and there would be no possibility of turning back. The people who had promised to repay me the money they owed had not shown up. In fact, in the previous two days they had seemed to disappear off the face of the earth. From my other friends – old friends who had not turned away from me despite my new faith, and who had promised to stand with me – no help came. And now here I was alone in the plane with nothing to my name but $100 and a one-way ticket to the other end of the globe.

'What's going to happen at the Bible school where I've promised to pay for my tuition and living expenses?' I wondered. A sense of panic seized me. 'What am I doing? Why am I doing this? It's not too late to turn back right now!'

I started to pray fervently. After a few moments, I remembered my dream. The peace of God descended upon me, and the Eternal One spoke softly into my heart. 'My daughter, which would you prefer – to travel with all the money and the comfort in the world without me, or to travel with me?' I could answer only that I chose him, my majestic King and heavenly Father.

I became immediately aware of the presence of the Holy Spirit with me so powerfully that I lost all anxieties; peace and joy filled my heart. I was travelling with the one to whom the whole world belonged – the King of kings. In this light, it wasn't important that I had almost nothing in my pocket. What was really important was that I had him, and that I was his beloved daughter: 'See what great love the Father has lavished on us, that we should be called children of God!' (1 John 3:1). He doesn't have any unloved children.

> The Spirit you received does not make you slaves, so that you live in fear again; rather, the Spirit you received brought about your adoption to sonship. And by him we cry, '*Abba*, Father.' The Spirit himself testifies with our spirit that we are God's children. Now if we are children, then we are heirs – heirs of God and

co-heirs with Christ, if indeed we share in his sufferings in order
that we may also share in his glory.

Romans 8:15–17

From that moment I simply enjoyed the wonderful trip accompanied by my heavenly Father. I didn't worry about anything
any more because it was clear to me that he was taking care of
everything. I felt joy and peace at each step along the way.

After arriving in Moscow I sent word to the Bible school in
South Africa that I was heading their way – but unfortunately
with almost no money. They responded that the Lord was leading me, and I should continue on: 'For we all belong to Christ
and are called to live by faith and utter dependence on him.'
Their response was extremely encouraging for me.

After staying in Moscow for a couple of days, I arrived in
Johannesburg, South Africa, on 12 January 2004. The pastor of
a local church met me at the airport and helped me get onto an
inter-city bus. This bus departed around five in the afternoon for
Bloemfontein where the CREARE International Bible School of
the Arts was located. I would arrive just before midnight.

The six-hour bus journey from Johannesburg to Bloemfontein became my first small, but unforgettable, introduction to
my new life in South Africa. It got dark shortly after we left
Johannesburg. Soon thereafter we were hit with a torrential
downpour. It seemed to me that a multitude of heavenly water
pumps were released on us all out of the dark sky, accompanied
by deafening thunderclaps and blinding lightning strikes. In
my whole life I had never seen anything like this. I was stunned
and terrified. It felt like the end of the world. Strangely enough,
no one else on the bus took much notice.

Slowly I calmed down. I began to pray fervently and shortly
afterwards the direction of my thinking completely altered.

'These are grandiose fireworks!' I thought. 'What beauty! My Father himself is welcoming me to this land with his fireworks!' Unspeakable joy, even ecstasy, filled my soul. When I looked at this spectacular display from the vantage point of peace and joy, it was so powerfully and supernaturally beautiful that it took my breath away. That night I had a window into the unmatched majesty and greatness of God. And I rejoiced with the knowledge that this great God had taken me by his hand.

So began my new life far from home. With some help I successfully found my way to my new school, where I was to study for the year 2004. That night, when they took me to the room where I was to stay, I wanted to cry. The room for seven women with rough iron bunk beds to sleep in reminded me of a room in the female prison I had visited for ministry in Temer-Kala in the months before my departure. I also quickly realized that my weak English was almost completely unintelligible to anyone in that building. And I could hardly understand a word they said.

I sat on my iron bed, feeling completely helpless and alone, and cried out to the Lord. 'Is this what you wanted for me? Lord, I don't understand anything that's being said. Would you, at least, speak to me? I really need you right now.'

I opened my Bible, and within moments my eyes fell on these words:

No one who has left home or brothers or sisters or mother or father or children or fields for me and the gospel will fail to receive a hundred times as much in this present age: homes, brothers, sisters, mothers, children and fields – along with persecutions – and in the age to come eternal life.

Mark 10:29,30

With this, God's peace returned to me. Encouragement directly from him – that was what I needed.

Both literally and figuratively CREARE became a 'school' for me of intense discipline and severe divine dealings. It was an effective place for the crucifixion of my old sinful nature with its strong ego, pride and stubbornness, and the raising up of a new nature after the character of Jesus; a wonderful place, where I could be restored – or broken.

In this place, I was no longer a famous superstar; I was nobody. I couldn't speak English. I didn't have any money. I didn't have any connections or close friends or relatives to lean on. The only thing I had was God. Someone once said that you'll never grasp how God is all you need until you are in a place where God is all you have. And here in South Africa I was exactly in that place; I had nothing and no one, except God.

The first three or four months were especially difficult. Without language, I had no meaningful relationship with any human being. All I could draw on was my relationship with the Lord himself. Praise God, you can fellowship with him in any language. He was literally the only one who understood me.

I loved spending time with God in the early morning hours. The school programme was packed full every day, so I got up at 4 o'clock to have three hours with the Lord before 7 a.m. I spent this time in prayer, in the Word, in worship and just in personal fellowship with him. I revelled in closeness and fellowship with my delightful Lord, looking forward to those times as keenly as a lover awaits her beloved. In these months my relationship with God and my faith grew in ways that I could never have dreamed of.

In that setting I was cut off from everything that was familiar. Everything that was comfortable to me was gone, and in their place were continual difficulties and trials. In the midst of this, I learned to listen to and notice the voice of God like never before. This became extremely precious to me.

There were times when I didn't know in the morning whether there would be money for my evening meal. Once I saw a girl in my dormitory throw half a bread roll into the garbage. It felt like a crime with so many around us in need. I waited for an opportune moment when no one was in the room and leapt to the garbage can, pulling out the bread roll and sprinting back to my chair. When I had caught my breath, I felt like a triumphant warrior who had captured a valuable trophy. My trophy tasted absolutely fantastic. It was no more than three or four bites along with a cup of tea, but I understood how a simple piece of bread with margarine can become a luxury when received with thankfulness.

One morning I went to church and all I had in my pocket – literally to my name – was about 40 rand (little more than £3). I had earned the money giving massages to some of my girl-friends. I was especially happy because I had been living by faith and this money would buy a little bread, tea, sugar and butter for the day. Suddenly I came to the conviction that the Lord wanted me to put all that money in the offering. At first this was hard to believe. All of it, God? But I love my God, and as a sign of my love, thankfulness and trust in him, I gave that money with joy.

The day after I had given the 40 rand in the offering, I was reading God's Word. As I read, it struck me strongly how important it is to not just seek to meet my own needs, but to serve others in *their* needs, especially those who are leaders in the household of faith. Why especially leaders? Well, because it's hardest of all for them – they are called to go forward and encounter most strongly the resistance and attacks of the enemy. On them lies an enormous weight of responsibility. I was filled with a sense that somehow I wanted to serve and help the pastor of our church. I thought, 'Maybe, I could even clean his home for him.' I prayed about this and asked the Lord to open the best way if this was what he wanted me to do. With that prayer in my heart, I went to the morning gathering without telling anyone.

At the end of the morning gathering, our pastor asked any to stand who would be willing to help him clean his home. I could not believe my ears. Our pastor had never made a request or announcement like that before. I stood. A number of other students also stood, responding to the pastor's request. Then the pastor asked, 'Who can help clean my house today, this evening after classes?' Everyone else sat down because it was a busy time in their schoolwork. I was the only one who remained standing. For me that evening was the only free evening in my entire week. Then the pastor announced that I would receive 1,000 rand (approximately £80). Everyone gasped. The pastor explained that the previous night the Holy Spirit woke him and instructed him to ask the students the following morning who would clean his home that evening, and give the one who responded 1,000 rand. My wonderful eternal God! How awesome and good he is! He always gives generously.

I also discovered the value of suffering in my years in South Africa. In the midst of tribulation I got to know the living God who turns everything for good for those who love him. I can testify to his faithfulness for the rest of my days. The Lord became even more real to me than the surrounding physical world.

> Not only so, but we also glory in our sufferings, because we know that suffering produces perseverance; perseverance, character; and character, hope. And hope does not put us to shame, because God's love has been poured out into our hearts through the Holy Spirit, who has been given to us.
>
> Romans 5:3–5

A human being can access freedom, joy and fullness of life only in the God who created him, and not through physical things or comforts. Step by step the eternal God freed me from dependence on the things of this world.

Was my life in this strange land difficult? Indeed it was! Extremely difficult. But at the same time, those difficulties were only for my good and led me to joy.

I didn't walk through these challenges alone. I honour with huge thankfulness my pastors and Christian leaders in South Africa. I also honour my fellow students, both in Bloemfontein and for the final two years at Hatfield Ministry Training School in Pretoria, where I also studied theology at Global University. Without their kindness so many times in so many ways, it would have been impossible. Many times the Lord worked through them, even when they may not have been aware of it, helping me through challenging days.

It was there in South Africa that I found freedom from my past emotional wounds, my self-centred patterns, my broken view of self, and much more. My whole life I had suffered from a tremendously damaged view of myself. But through the Lord's ministry in South Africa, I was finally able to accept myself as a precious creation of God. I came to believe that the Lord had made me as I was and had given me unique gifts and potential. I started to see myself in a totally new way.

The creative side of my personality opened up for the first time. I had always sung songs, but now I found myself able to actually compose songs from my heart. To my joy I received one of the highest scores at CREARE for my musical composition. What a confirmation this was of the newness and freedom inside! Even in dancing I found new freedom. What amazement and encouragement when I witnessed tears in the eyes of my instructor as I performed a dance routine of my own creation.

The Holy Spirit used the art classes powerfully. Dance, drama or other classes often turned into awesome experiences of God, healing or deliverance for many students. Through art I met my real self as God extricated me from the false and negative concepts about myself that had developed in me. I found that I was chained by complexes and defeatist thoughts.

In one drama session, God revealed himself in such a real way and I felt his love so powerfully that it became excruciatingly painful. A blast of enormous pain came out of the past. Bitterness of heart seized me, and I told God that I did not need his love: 'After a lifetime of being deprived of love, I can get along without it.'

A minister approached with communion, but I could not accept it because anger and resentment filled me. Only then did I realize the extent to which such bitterness lurked in the innermost parts of my soul. I cried and screamed, 'Leave me alone! I don't need anything from anyone!' The Lord waited patiently with outstretched hands; he understood that this was my severe pain, not renunciation of him.

As I mentioned earlier, I had always had a terrible fear of speaking in public. Even in fairly small circles, I felt insecure and inept. As I grew up in my village, some of the adults would cut me off when I tried to say something. Only stupidities came out of mouth, they said, and it would be better if I kept my mouth shut. I came to believe what was said about me and developed a deep complex. For years I would be nervous even at the dinner table, not knowing what to do with my hands or my eyes, how to behave or what to say. Sometimes my face flushed with embarrassment because of my nervousness. If I tried to say something, I would be sure that what came out of my mouth was stupid. It seemed that no matter how hard I tried, I could never make any progress in overcoming these fears. The best I could do was to cover my inner struggles, hiding behind masks and screens.

It was only when I gave my heart to Jesus and turned to him that I started to see myself through his eyes, so full of love and purity. I gradually started seeing myself as the long-closed petals of a flower; he was the warm, healing sun. In the rays of his love, the beauty of this flower opened. Only the true God can free a person from the lies which have built up over many years.

About six months after my arrival in South Africa I was able to joyfully give a fifteen-minute talk in English about my life to a group of young people at a university youth group. I told them how the Lord had saved me and set me free. Many of these young people came up to me afterwards and described how the Holy Spirit had worked in them through my talk. What a joy this was to me! What a confirmation of the freedom God had given me! He is able to take the weakest and most unattractive areas of our lives and use them for his glory in ministering life to other people.

Another talk I gave was later on, when I was asked to speak in front of a large congregation in Pretoria. As I told of God's work in my life, I saw that the pastor was moved to tears. Later he shared that he was amazed to hear that one year earlier I had not been able to speak at all in English. He concluded that it was only possible because of the work of Christ in me because speaking fluently and powerfully in a new language in such a short time is not normally possible. Yet when I started to speak of the awesome working of the Lord, the words flowed from my mouth like a river of living water. With God, the one whom I love and serve, nothing is impossible! Praise to him for his wonderful work of setting me free.

8

Sharing Love

As the months went by, my longing for my homeland became stronger and stronger. I had never wanted to live overseas. To take a short trip is one thing, but to reside in a foreign country for a long period of time is completely different. No matter where I travelled or how wonderful the people were, I yearned to return to Russia and my home region. I especially longed to see my native mountains, the Caucasus. I sent letters to my mother and to others, but for a long time I didn't get any answers. I was so homesick that I would often turn on my little CD player and listen to music from my Caucasus region and cry. After an interminably long stretch, letters started coming from my mother. And then some letters from two sisters in the Lord from my home church back in Temer-Kala. I was overjoyed with these letters.

Approximately a year into my time in South Africa, a letter arrived from one of my younger sisters. I was so happy that I couldn't wait to open it, but when I started to read, the letter cut me to the quick. Her blunt words went on and on, accusing me with the most malicious words you could choose. I was baffled because I hadn't done anything negative towards her or her family. My terrible wrong was basically that I had chosen to love Jesus and follow him. With where I was emotionally,

I couldn't protect my heart from this assault, and the attack of the evil one through these words hurt me deeply. I felt like a critically wounded bird, and at least a month went by before I could even start to recover emotionally.

Out of the blue one day, I remembered these words from the New Testament:

> I have come in my Father's name, and you do not accept me; but if someone else comes in his own name, you will accept him. How can you believe since you accept glory from one another but do not seek the glory that comes from the only God?'
>
> John 5:43,44

It's paradoxical that when I pursued glory for myself, the world readily accepted me, and my family and close friends rejoiced. But when I started to seek God's glory, I became, at best, uninteresting – and at worst, a fully fledged traitor.

It took a long time before I could recover emotional strength and answer my sister. I wrote back to her in God's love, thanking her for her honesty, and expressing my sorrow that I had caused her such pain. God's Spirit gave me wisdom and peace in my heart about my relationship with my sister. I thank him for this and for all the ways he helped me in that time! With this peace in my heart, I prayed even more fervently for my unsaved family members, asking God to give me opportunities to serve my sister and show her how much God loved her in ways she could understand.

Four months later, the huge desire to travel back to my homeland stirred again within me. But a trip to southern Russia would have cost at least 40,000 roubles (approximately £530). I was far from having that kind of money. However, stirred by faith, I went to the travel bureau and ordered some tickets.

They gave me two days to pay at that price. I gave myself to prayer that God's will be done in this.

The next day my friend Melisha came to me unexpectedly. She said that the Lord had led her to give me some money for the airfare home. She knew nothing about my thoughts on this or about the step I had taken the previous day. It was a divine miracle! Melisha rarely came to visit me, but on those unusual occasions when she appeared, it was always accompanied by some holy act of God. The Holy Spirit worked powerfully through her. I was speechless with joy at God's provision for me to travel home to my native land.

When I arrived home, the sister who had written to me was soon due to give birth – a fact that no one had mentioned. Furthermore, my sister had no women around her who could help her. I rejoiced in the Lord's timing and pitched in to help her in every way that I could.

My sister was certain that she was going to give birth to a son, but the Holy Spirit inspired me to say that the baby would be a girl, and that this girl would become a huge blessing for their family. That is exactly what happened. Many times in the years following, my sister has expressed that she didn't know what she would have done without the help and blessing of this daughter.

After that it was like the letter had never happened. My relationship with my sister wonderfully improved. She is a sincerely good-hearted person, who strives to do what is right. I respect her, and I continue to believe that at some point, the light of truth in Jesus will penetrate her heart. Then she will understand all that the Lord has done.

Do not be overcome by evil, but overcome evil with good.

Romans 12:21

Back in South Africa, I was now studying at Hatfield Ministry Training School in Pretoria. A group of us went on a mission trip to Lesotho, a small independent country completely surrounded by South Africa. The population is almost entirely black and extremely poor. Homes do not have electricity or running water, and many of them are even without outdoor toilets. For the most part, the spiritual condition of the Sotho people is even worse. Witchcraft and occult practices are pervasive. Due to moral degeneracy combined with lack of education, AIDS is rampant and devastating. The country suffers from a high mortality rate among young adults, resulting in many orphaned children.

Our team planned to serve in compassion ministries during the day alongside some long-term mission workers. Each of us would live with a local family and stay in those homes at night. Before leaving Pretoria, we prayed together that the Lord would give us comfortable and well-equipped accommodations. We were worried about how poor, primitive and unsanitary Lesotho was reputed to be. One possibility was to stay in the well-appointed homes of the expatriate missionaries.

The hour we arrived something inside me rebelled against this prayer. I told the Lord, 'On this trip I want to fulfil your will – the exact plans you have sent me here for – and so I retract my prayer and ask you to do exactly that, no matter what it costs me.'

The rest of the group were assigned families of an upper income bracket. Except me. I landed in a family of orphans headed by a sixteen-year-old girl. It was the cold season of the year. The children cooked over an open fire in the centre of the room. The first time I entered the little hut, I nearly passed out from the thick smoke. Their primary food day after day was a kind of porridge prepared from corn flour and water. Every evening the oldest girl cooked the porridge and fed her circle of half-clothed, barefoot younger children. Following this 'meal' they all lay down to sleep on threadbare blankets laid out on the cold floor. They gave me their only bed, since I was their guest. The cold intensified during the night. In addition to the sleeping bag I had brought, I threw around me my two reserve blankets, trying to keep warm.

That first evening, sitting in the dark with my eyes watering from the smoke, unable even to read since there was no electricity, I gave in to a deep feeling of despondency. From time to time, a young drunken man stopped to look through the door at everyone. That felt uncomfortable. During the night, I thought many times, 'Missionary service is definitely not for me.' Then again, 'Lord, how could I be of any real help here anyway? What could I change? What's the point of even being here?' I didn't feel like I had anything to offer. What, if anything, could I do? I felt so feeble.

I thought back to all the difficulties I had experienced growing up in poverty, then living for a while in luxury. Now I only wanted to serve the Lord in a straightforward way without any more drama. I fell asleep in complete discouragement, thinking, 'I don't want to be a missionary. Tomorrow I'll leave this place.'

But the next morning I woke up with these words from the Bible running through my spirit: '"What should we do then?" the crowd asked. John answered, "Anyone who has two shirts should share with the one who has none, and anyone who has food should do the same"' (Luke 3:10,11).

I began to pray. It felt like a miracle because I soon saw everything from a totally different perspective. Joy appeared in my heart because the Lord had spoken to me, and I could see exactly what I could do for these young orphans. That afternoon I returned to this home with bags of food I had purchased with the bit of money in my pocket. I had enough for a loaf of bread, a jar of jam and some butter, along with a packet of tea and some sugar, some peanut butter and apples. It felt like a feast in the little hut that night.

I planned to give these children everything I had brought with me when I left in a couple of days, including the blankets and sleeping bag. But when I set out to give them everything materially I could, the Lord opened my eyes again. He showed me that I had a lot more to give if I opened my heart. I could give them myself – my time, my love, my attention and my fellowship.

It was so simple! How had I not seen this before? I expected something complicated, but the Holy Spirit suggested something simple. I spent a glorious time with these children, and the Holy Spirit was free to work among us.

I began by telling them about my own life in far-away Russia and about the beautiful mountains of my home region. Later we conversed about the great Father God and his love for each of us. When I began to tell them in detail about this amazing God who had created each one of them and loved them, they listened with bated breath. I told them that God had a beautiful plan for each of their lives, and that he would provide for them. As they began to see this, they listened with wide-eyed attention, and when I started to sing, they came alive! Jumping up, they interrupted each other, sharing their future dreams and hopes. Then they all began dancing and singing. I love African songs and dancing. Their performance that night – despite the dim, squalid hut – brought me overflowing joy.

One of the younger brothers was extremely ill. He lay on a little cot in the corner. The oldest sister said he had been sick for almost two weeks. When I prayed for him, accompanied by the other children, he stood up and danced a lively African dance all around the room. The next day, when I left, he was completely healthy and stood at the doorway of the hut to wave goodbye to me. All praise to the Lord!

God spoke to me during that trip, showing me that many people want to see God's miraculous power at work in and through them. We often pray for this. The Lord hears these prayers and opens to us possibilities for cooperation with him. However, we frequently baulk at uncomfortable, difficult circumstances, and so we lose the opportunities God is giving us. I am thankful to God that he helped me to see his hand in the midst of that situation so that I could share in the joy of his power at work. Those dear children will never forget how the great God once sent to them a young woman from far-off Russia to show them how much he loves them and tell them of his good plan for their lives.

I left Lesotho with my heart overflowing with joy, knowing that those precious children now had a personal connection with Jesus – their very best and most faithful Friend. He personally loves them and, thanks to him, they can go forward with real hope, knowing that he will work in their lives and help his dreams and their dreams be fulfilled.

The Holy Spirit spoke to me in those days and made it clear that if a person only wants comfort, then physical comfort is the most they will receive. On the other hand, if a person wants God and they are prepared to place their life in total availability to him, that person will gain the fullness of God and all his love and power that goes with it. I came back from that trip a different person. I had only one desire – to pass on to others what the Lord had kindly given me in that time. All glory and praise to the generous God who invites us to cooperate with him!

Here are some living words that the Holy Spirit gave through his servant, Paul:

But whatever were gains to me I now consider loss for the sake of Christ. What is more, I consider everything a loss because of the surpassing worth of knowing Christ Jesus my Lord, for whose sake I have lost all things. I consider them garbage, that I may gain Christ and be found in him, not having a righteousness of my own that comes from the law, but that which is through faith in Christ – the righteousness that comes from God on the basis of faith. I want to know Christ – yes, to know the power of his resurrection and participation in his sufferings, becoming like him in his death, and so, somehow, attaining to the resurrection from the dead.

Philippians 3:7–11

9

The Truest Love

When you ask people as to which sphere of their life represents the most difficult area for them, the answers are remarkably varied: finances, career, family, health, emotions, male-female relationships. The toughest area for me was that last one on the list. I would hold in contempt those who fell in love with me. And those with whom I fell in love often seemed to disappear.

About a year after my conversion, and after everything had ended with Gadzhi, I'd met Richard, an American Christian who came to the North Caucasus for missionary service, and he declared his love to me. At the start of 2002, I had been invited to America – by Richard – where I travelled to many churches, giving my testimony and singing. I had a translator with me because at that time I could not speak English. Richard convinced me that God had spoken to him and said that I was the right one for him, and that it was God's will for us to marry. Richard had been a Christian for twenty years by that time. I was a new convert and looked on Christians – especially experienced Christians, as I considered Richard to be – through rose-tinted glasses. So I trusted his every word.

I responded with agreement. From childhood, my most fervently held dream had been a loving family with happy children. Although I had many fans, my dream of marriage had never materialized. It almost seemed like I was cursed. Now there was nothing to fear; finally a wonderful married life awaited me. Not only was Richard a believer, but he was a person of maturity and ministry experience. Everything within me longed for a stable and trustworthy relationship. How wonderful to have this loving Christian man by my side, mature in the Lord and spiritually strong! We would pray together, study God's Word together, and serve the Lord. In my naivety, I supposed that everything from here on would be endlessly glorious.

I had always been excessively romantic, and suffered as a result. If I gave my heart to someone, I did it sincerely, 100 per cent, without any scheming or trickery. I simply couldn't live without love. But I had such strong internal needs and could never find peace or satisfaction. The catastrophic deficit of love inside my soul left me unprepared to develop a healthy mutual relationship and led me time after time to tragic ends.

In Richard, I thought I had met a man who loved me just as I was. We travelled together to America in Christian circles, even visited Hollywood and other scenic places. There in California he proposed to me in an unforgettably beautiful setting. But days after our engagement, he got cold feet. Or maybe there was something about me that scared him off. In any case, he announced that he had rushed into things and wanted to end our relationship. It was a nightmare. A few days later he apologized. He said that he really loved me and didn't know why he had behaved like that. By then I was completely confused and had no idea what to expect.

Upon my return to Russia, I wrote to him from Moscow. I was worn out by the instability and uncertainty that had overtaken our relationship. Maybe it would be better to remain friends and bring our romantic relationship to an end. To this suggestion, he responded, it seemed to me, almost eagerly; and that was that.

My heart was broken. I came close to leaving the church. If believing Christians could act like this, what was the difference from the rest of the world? And who needs a church with people like this!

Through the trauma I came to see that believers are still just people with their weaknesses and mistakes. Only Jesus is perfectly trustworthy. I also realized that it would be wrong to judge an entire church based on the immature actions of a few individuals.

I did not take the break-up well. It was only in God that I found any comfort. I drew strength from his love, and this kept me from plunging to even further depths. As I look back, I can thank the Lord for using this time to begin the freeing work of deep cleansing inside me.

Four years later, a second more severe trial in this area awaited me in South Africa. In our church in Pretoria I had become acquainted with a young man whom I will call John. He was a very interesting person, outstanding in many ways. He touched my heart with his beautiful manner towards me. Before long our relationship took a strong romantic turn, and we became engaged.

John created an unforgettable evening in preparation for his proposal. I was overwhelmed by his love and kindness and fully ready to say yes. He gave me the most beautiful diamond ring. I can't put into words how touched I was. I saw the hand of God in this and God's blessing on our relationship. I was so happy and full of joyful hope for the future.

We were set to be married in a few months, but problems surfaced. On the one hand, we were drawn towards each other and both wanted to marry as soon as possible. But quarrels, irritations and misunderstandings became more and more frequent. I lost all peace in my heart, but I couldn't bear the thought of the relationship breaking up. John also feared ending the engagement. We genuinely loved one another. Finally I suggested that we step back for a period of time and give each other some space. I wanted to pray and sort things out within myself in order to find the Lord's will afresh for me. John agreed, and I decided to travel home to Russia for a month.

We had several outstanding pastors in our church there in Pretoria. They had conducted our pre-marriage counselling sessions. With their maturity and pastoral experience, they saw things that at the moment I could not (and did not want to) see. Just before I left for Russia, two of the pastors invited me to meet at a café. There they urged me to think seriously about whether this relationship with John was what the Lord wanted for me. They reminded me of God's calling on my life and questioned whether that calling could go forward if my life were joined with John's.

I respected their opinion, but I still did not want to think about breaking off the relationship. We had come so far. The wedding date was already set. 'Even if there are difficulties later,' I thought, 'John and I have grown to know each other really well.' Besides, I was in love.

While I was in Russia, John called me often, and we prayed together over the phone. I set aside a three-day fast to seek the Lord about the right direction for our relationship. Everything that I heard from the Lord seemed to say that I should give John the time he needed and the freedom to independently decide about this.

On the phone, I told him what I was sensing. I continued to ask the Lord to help John to make the right decision. In the depths of my being I hoped that his decision would be positive. During these weeks at home I gradually became more and more peaceful about the relationship. Confident of the outcome, before I returned to South Africa, I told my family and friends about my upcoming wedding.

John met me at the airport, but a surprise awaited me – a surprise that I had greatly feared deep down. With the help of the Lord and our precious pastors, he had come to the decision that it was right to end our relationship. My heart seemed to fall out of my body.

I returned that beautiful ring, but this trial rapidly consumed me like a fire. I simply wasn't prepared for the convulsions of soul that I went through. Although I had submitted to God's voice and had given John the freedom to say yes or no, when he actually said a firm no, it felt like I was cut in half. Of course, it would not have been as emotionally devastating if I had been the one to say no to him, but the fact that this man I loved had ended it with me felt like the sting of vinegar poured into a bleeding, raw wound.

'Haven't I suffered enough already? This is so cruel! Why is this happening to me now, when I'm following you, Lord?' These are the questions I poured out to God. I didn't even wait for answers. Like a wounded bird, I felt like I had nowhere to go. The ocean of pain I had been storing within like a reservoir for years burst violently through the dam. In the process, the torrent swept away all my masks and protective 'fig leaves'. Only God could help me find resolution.

There were many evenings in those weeks I went into the orchard nearby, after classes and studying, to kneel before the Lord. With no words even to pray, sometimes psalms came, asking God to preserve me from despair and depression. Day after day he gave me strength and encouragement sufficient for that day so that I could go on while he accomplished his precious cleansing work within me. In the midst of pain and tears I reminded myself that I was persevering with his help so that I would come out like gold refined through the fire. The one thing I knew was that I was in God's hands and that he loved me. He would never forsake me even though some days this was hard to feel.

In the following months I often cried out to the Lord with these words from his holy Word – words which previously I had been hesitant to even voice out loud:

Though the fig-tree does not bud
    and there are no grapes on the vines,
though the olive crop fails
    and the fields produce no food,
though there are no sheep in the sheepfold
    and no cattle in the stalls,
yet I will rejoice in the LORD,
    I will be joyful in God my Saviour.
The Sovereign LORD is my strength;
    he makes my feet like the feet of a deer,
    he enables me to tread on the heights.

Habakkuk 3:17–19

The work was a deep excavation, major internal surgery, extremely painful, but very necessary.

I began a forty-day period of fasting, taking nothing but water during the day and some light refreshment in the evening, in order to pray for my cleansing and internal healing. These verses from Psalm 139 occupied the central place in my prayers:

Search me, God, and know my heart;
    test me and know my anxious thoughts.

See if there is any offensive way in me,
    and lead me in the way everlasting.

Psalm 139:23,24

One day the Eternal One spoke to me: 'My blood cannot cover what you keep hiding. How can you say that you trust me if you fear what people think more than you fear me?'

When I first gave my life to my beloved Lord Jesus, I thought that everything in my past was forgiven and gone and I would never have to speak about it to anyone. Indeed, it says that old things are passed away; everything has become new (see 2 Corinthians 5:17). Honestly, in the early years I didn't understand the full meaning of this verse.

Because the internal pain in my soul didn't just go away, I continued to respond with unhealthy patterns. I did not have a well-grounded emotional stability. Although much had changed for the better in my life, I wasn't experiencing anything approaching the fullness of well-being which the Lord had promised in his Word.

One of our Bible school teachers said, 'Our dear Lord says to each one of his children, "Everything inside that you keep hidden in the darkness, the devil is able to use against you."' These words caused me to seriously stop and think.

'But if I tell another human being everything that has happened to me . . . How could I possibly speak out loud such horribly shameful things?' It seemed to me that I would never be able to do that.

Stronghold of pride! It held me captive to the darkness of lies, not allowing me to welcome my own personal freedom. But when the Eternal One himself spoke to me about this, something clicked. I began to feel the flame of hope, and understood that I had to break through this 'I can't'. I had to overcome this enemy of pride if I wanted to take hold of full freedom in Christ. God strengthened me with the following truth from his Word:

> If we claim to have fellowship with him and yet walk in the darkness, we lie and do not live out the truth. But if we walk in the light, as he is in the light, we have fellowship with one another, and the blood of Jesus, his Son, purifies us from all sin. If we claim to be without sin, we deceive ourselves and the truth is not in us. If we confess our sins, he is faithful and just and will forgive us our sins and purify us from all unrighteousness.
>
> 1 John 1:6–9

These words were revealed to me with new power and depth. The old pride, now exposed to the light, began to lose its hold on me.

Jesus was not ashamed to take all of my (and your) sin and shame on himself. He did this publicly, before the eyes of the whole world, on the cross on the hill of Golgotha so that you and I could be free. There was nothing left to be ashamed of. All that remained was to take the darkness, bring it to the light and give it to him. Darkness is only defeated by light. And where everything is in the light, there is total freedom.

In order to find healing for a serious illness, you must first acknowledge the illness and allow doctors to prescribe a course of treatment. It's impossible to be free from pain if you aren't willing to let the abscess be cleansed. In the same way, it's not possible to be freed from the damaging effects of sin if you don't acknowledge and expose that sin to the light.

To be crucified with Christ, we must cast away all of our 'fig leaves' of pride which we put up as masks in front of others. That is, we must honestly expose our weakness. The problem is that none of us wants to do that, even though we long for the power of God to work in our lives. But there is no painless cure for the extrication of damaging past sin from the soul. That which a person keeps back in the darkness will always work against him and bring ugly results.

By the grace of God, exactly when I was dealing with this most severe area of struggle following my break-up with John, a major class began in the Bible school on 'Counselling for Christian Growth and Inner Healing'. This class was led by a wonderful woman, wholly consecrated to God, with many years of effective experience in restoration counselling ministry. She began to hold individual counselling sessions with me. This was necessary before I could help others in ministry.

For the first time in my life, with the help of God's Word and thanks to God's provision of this woman, I was able to bring to the light many things from my past that for years I had hidden under the 'necessary' cover of darkness. It took many hours of ministry to pour out the buried darkness of my past life. I literally gasped for breath sometimes from the pain of talking about these things. This experienced servant of God patiently listened and prayed for me as I dug out portion after portion of infection. The poison I had long carried in the depths of my soul had corroded my insides. But now I was determined to get it all out, and I had a trustworthy minister of grace with me.

When all of this decay was finally brought into the light and replaced with grace and truth, the pain inside started to go away. It's hard to find words to describe how 'light' I felt, how free after so many years of carrying the weight. Praise to you, my amazing Lord! He not only saves us from judgment in his wonderful grace, but he heals our wounded souls and restores the damaged areas to fullness of life. The past, the present and the future all belong to him, and he wants to heal us completely.

Therefore confess your sins to each other and pray for each other so that you may be healed. The prayer of a righteous person is powerful and effective.

James 5:16

The past is part of your life, and you can't ignore it, or pretend to forget it. There is no point in scorning it, and you don't need to fear it. If you don't deal with your past in a healthy manner, it will stalk you like some invisible, insidious enemy, tormenting your soul.

The devil uses various tactics to keep people in bondage: religiosity, super-spirituality, pride, shame, judgment, fear, unresolved hate and other similar binding factors. But God sets people free through faith, humility, forgiveness and *agape* love. The devil wants everything to stay hidden in the dark. God pulls off the curtain of darkness and fills our lives with cleansing, healing, light and freedom. The devil says, 'Destroy.' God says, 'Save.'

Shortly after I came to Jesus, I wondered, 'Why couldn't I have come to him sooner? I would have avoided so many mistakes.' But I came to understand that although he wanted me to come to him as soon as possible, he was able to redeem even this. It was only when I came to total brokenness and humility that I was able to respond to him. Now I truly have a true understanding of grace when I see how he has been able to forgive and redeem all of the past darkness. This redemption gives me greater understanding and compassion for others trapped in sin. He took my hard, stone-like heart and changed it into a heart that was capable of love, forgiveness and heartfelt compassion. Previously, judgment and criticism came naturally to me. Now, in Jesus, that became unnatural and repulsive. I can never forget the terrible hole from which his hand of mercy pulled me. As a result, I can extend a hand of mercy to those who are lost.

Having passed through this intense stage of trial and inner restoration, at last I truly understood that getting married wasn't what I needed. What I needed was to receive inner healing and freedom in the Lord, rather than seeking comfort from without. When I realized this, that old deep feeling of loneliness and unhealthy neediness began to fall away. I didn't need a man constantly with me to be OK. My relationship with John had been based on physical attraction and my deep need to have someone there with me, not on pure love. We were two wounded people, continually rewounding each other. Our married life would have been full of huge needs and conflicts. I was no more prepared for successful family life than I was when I had been with Richard. When I was set free from the heavy weights of the past, I came to know a closeness to my marvellous Creator and a wholeness in myself that I had not known before. I tasted real freedom. With all my heart, I now thank my heavenly Father that he protected me from marrying John. I hope and pray that John has also found happiness and well-being in his personal life.

When I was still engaged to John, I heard a great servant of the Lord preach God's Word. He told about a time when he was led to lay down before the Lord every right in his life, including the right to be married. His life changed in amazing ways. At the end of his message, he challenged everyone present to take the same step. At that moment I knew the Lord was speaking to me. I had a choice. I looked down at the ring on my finger and thought deeply. Was I willing to give it up?

I really wished God to bless my union with John. 'I'll soon turn forty; and getting married and raising a family has been the central dream of my life! If I turn away now, there will be no more chances. I'll remain single. And I am so weary of people asking when I am going to get married!' With all of these emotions pouring through me, my flesh rebelled against the thought of giving up marriage to John. In front of me I saw only the gloomiest, most depressing future without him.

Nonetheless, that evening, I stood up. I told the Lord that although I very much wanted to marry John and keep this ring, I wanted more than anything else to fulfil his will. I gave the Lord all my rights and invited him to do whatever was best for my life – even if that meant not marrying John. 'If it is necessary to go through difficult times, so be it – just so that, whatever it takes, you fulfil your will in my life.'

God heard me. He always responds to heartfelt prayers. To end up away from the will of God would be a hundred times more awful than any trial necessary to walk through with him. That which seemed to me to be a wrenching, disgraceful episode of brokenness – ending a relationship when engaged is shameful for a woman in my culture, and this had now happened to me twice – turned into the most triumphal victory for me. And this came about, not due to the strength of human will, but the strength of humility in the power of his love. When I let God bring me to full submission and full trust in his will, the power of his love came alive in me.

10

The Father's Love

Shortly after this momentous time, I felt the Holy Spirit leading me to a ten-day total fast. He was calling me to a closer relationship with him, to seek his will in my life. I was concerned specifically about his choice for a future life partner for me. I didn't want to commit further mistakes regarding this question. After my relationship with Richard and before meeting John, I had seriously considered whether the Lord was leading me to remain celibate for the rest of my life, but God did not confirm this. He had his own very best plan for me. I must wait on him for the right partner.

I also needed a breakthrough in the area of finances. A large sum of money was due for my study expenses. In my years in the Lord, he had always looked out for me, amazingly providing what was needed, time after time. Usually this provision came without my even needing to ask. I sought to be obedient to his direction, and he took care of my needs. But in the previous three or four months it seemed that God had closed all the channels of my financial provision. My prayers about this didn't seem to go beyond the ceiling of my room. This time of testing was especially difficult because it came alongside the painful ending of my relationship with John. I was tempted to think that God had rejected me and no longer loved me.

Objectively, I knew this wasn't the truth. But our feelings often lead us into deep, dark pits. I couldn't understand what was going on, but I did know what God's Word said:

> And we know that in all things God works for the good of those
> who love him, who have been called according to his purpose.
>
> Romans 8:28

In the midst of a classroom session after many weeks of bewilderment, suffering, constant prayer, and what seemed like total silence from God's side, I heard the gentle voice of the Holy Spirit clearly saying that through these circumstances he wanted to raise me up to new levels of faith. My joy knew no bounds! The Lord was speaking to me! This was by far the most important thing. I was as happy as a little child who had been lost and then their parents found them.

A few days later I received notice that some money had been deposited in my account – the equivalent of £380. This was a huge sum of money for me in a time when I was living with almost no funds. That was the first time I cried from pure joy. The joy came from knowing that I was in God's hands. He would never forget me, never leave me, and never be late.

But the Lord had still more surprises for me. Within a day or two of the time I received that money, I dreamed a vivid dream about one of the girl students in our school. In the dream, she desperately needed funds. I knew this girl. The Lord had given her a calling to serve in the one of the poorest regions of South Africa. In prayer in the dream I received crystal clear understanding that the Lord wanted me to give her the £380 I had received.

'Why me, Lord?' My education fees were growing bigger, and I needed all that money! But the Lord was clear. I went to the girl. And she was in desperate need of that exact sum of money – £380.

I don't know who was more full of joy, she for the Lord answering her prayer exactly and amazingly, or me that God had entrusted me with this holy task. When we both saw the powerful actions of the living God working through us, we were filled with faith.

A few more weeks went by, and my financial situation was unchanged. My school debt continued to grow. At this point I got the clear sense that I should fast. During a time of fervent prayer, the Holy Spirit helped me determine the beginning and length for this particular fast. This was one of the most difficult fasts in all my Christian life. I knew that I was not to eat anything for the whole ten days. I had never attempted a total fast for that length of time. Previously such fasts had been between one and seven days.

Along with fierce hunger pangs I experienced excruciating pain all over my body. This searing pain only subsided on the eighth day. On the ninth day I was beset with a splitting headache, which only diminished late in the evening after the believers prayed for me. But I had a strong inner conviction that the Lord had led me to this fast and that he was accomplishing important things in the spiritual realm through it. This knowledge steeled my resolve through the hunger and pain. My hunger for God was so strong that while writhing in pain with tears streaming down my face, I called out to the Lord repeatedly, 'I want you and your will in my life far more than I want to assuage this pain and hunger!'

The Lord wonderfully spoke to me during this time of fasting and prayer. Almost every night I was awakened by his voice. Here are some of the things he said during those days:

'Flee from religiosity.'

'I am your God, El-Shaddai. You will not be in need of anything. I will saturate you with my blessings out of my treasure house.'

'My Word is within you.'

'Call unto me, and I will answer you and show you great and mighty things that you know not' (see Jeremiah 33:3).

From the early days of my conversion to Christ, fasting and prayer had been a way of life for me. Here again its value was confirmed. The action of God in my life that followed fasting has not always been what I wanted or expected. Most of all it draws us near to God so that he can make things clear in his relationship with us. When his will becomes clear, it is so much simpler to triumph over personal desires. The things that seemed so important before the fast often become less of an issue in the light of God's presence. And you're empowered to overcome difficulties and trials with renewed vigour. Fasting and prayer cleanses and quiets the soul. It changes your focus, making you sensitive to the Holy Spirit.

A noticeable thing that happened in me after this ten-day fast was an overflow of divine love towards other people. I could hardly walk past people on the street. My eyes had been opened and I saw other human beings in a new way. Love for the lost overwhelmed me. This came about in me after these times of prayer and fasting and also in connection with the major healing that had happened inside my heart.

As a result of this fast, I received absolute peace regarding God's provision and plan for my personal life. I could now rest in the knowledge that the Lord had the right future marriage partner for me and that this would come about in God's time.

The Lord also answered in regard to finances. A few days after the completion of this ten-day fast I was sweeping the floor in my room. Suddenly I saw a vision like a waterfall, but it was a cascade of hundreds of banknotes in different currencies and denominations. At that moment I knew that all the financial provision I needed was on the way, and in abundance.

A little later I received another confirmation. Early one morning I was in the prayer room at the church near the Bible school. Usually no one interacted with me during these quiet prayer times. I had never seen anyone receive a prophetic utterance there, but that morning a highly respected elderly Christian brother came up to me. With prophetic anointing he said, 'Shaadia, God wants to bless you very generously. Accept that he will give to you not only generously, but super-generously.'

I was almost in shock with joy. I had not the slightest doubt that this word had come from the Lord.

Then following all this, two or three more long months went by with no visible change in my financial situation. Only a miracle could help me now. My faith started to feel like a boat rocked in a storm. At times it seemed I was sinking almost to the bottom of the sea; then suddenly I would lurch upward to the peak of a wave. As a boat is tested for sturdiness through a storm, my faith was being severely tested. But eventually all storms come to an end and peaceful, sunny days do arrive.

One day my friend Melisha told me that her husband had bought a new car and given his old car to her. When she prayed about what to do, she decided to bless me with her old Mercedes. She and her husband felt in their hearts that this was what the Lord wanted them to do. In the days and weeks following I received multiple phone calls, one after another, from various friends telling me about financial gifts they were giving me. Individually they each said that this was what the Lord had moved them to do.

That promised waterfall had actually arrived, and my faith was greatly strengthened. God blessed me so generously that at one point I said to him, 'Lord, what am I supposed to do with all this?' My dreams and prayers had gone no further than to pay my school debt, buy the plane ticket home, and have a little money left over for expenses on the road. But God gave me far more than that.

I totally paid off all school expenses, bought the things that I needed, and was even able to help some of the other students who were in similar situations to me. Finally, after all that, I bought a computer. When you entrust everything to him, life with Jesus is sheer thrilling adventure. He loves to create happy surprises.

> If you, then, though you are evil, know how to give good gifts to your children, how much more will your Father in heaven give good gifts to those who ask him!
>
> Matthew 7:11

At the time I began my new life in Christ, my previous experience with my earthly father had been extremely negative and sad. How could I consider a loving, close, trusting relationship with someone who called himself 'Father'? My soul overflowed with bitterness and offence at my earthly father. Even to think about him was difficult for me. This interfered with various aspects of my life. God started working inner healing directly in this sphere of enormous pain. I would be dishonest if I didn't say that it was a very painful process.

God gently and patiently led me into this. He began teaching me to look at my father in a completely new way, and ultimately to look at myself in a new way. I began to find healing. Little by little my feelings regarding my father changed. I started to forgive him and to love him with a genuine love. Concurrently, my relationship with my heavenly Father progressed. Nonetheless, at times I still felt barriers in my soul that

kept me from fullness of life and wholeness in my relationship with God the Father and with people. Sometimes I simply
couldn't get a handle on my emotions. Sadness would almost
engulf me. In those moments I cried out to God, 'Lord, I know
that you love me, that I'm forgiven. Why do I still feel so bad?'

During my studies in South Africa, one instructor empha-
sized how important forgiveness was. He said that it was necessary to forgive others, forgive ourselves, and even forgive God.
I couldn't believe my ears. Are you serious – forgive God? But
it turns out that it actually is possible. It's not that God needs
our forgiveness, but we're the ones that need to work through
our unresolved bitterness. He was, is, and will forever remain
the Holy One, totally irreproachable and pure. He has no sin
that needs forgiving. But we need to work through to grace.

This revelation that I could and needed to forgive God,
my heavenly Father, became a huge spiritual breakthrough
and ultimately revolutionized my whole relationship with
God. Equally stunning and significant was the realization that
I could and should express to God all that I was feeling – even
my ugly feelings of frustration and hate.

I walked out of that Bible class stirred by what I had heard.
I climbed a little hill next to the church to pray. Suddenly
I was consumed with inner indignation, feeling deeply offended
at God, and an intense resistance to calling him 'Father'. I almost screamed at God, pouring out my pain, hurt, anger, hate,
hardly able to catch my breath in the midst of my tears. Up until
that moment I could not have conceived that such anger at God
was hiding inside me. Or that it was this, more than anything
else, that kept me from 'spreading my wings' in spiritual growth.
Undoubtedly, he knew. He, in his amazing mercy and love, decided through this means to set me free from this vile and deadly
dangerous inner weight which I had been dragging around.

'You want to say that you are my Father? You mean *really* a father? Well, where were you when I was going through all that suffering?' I had never spoken to my father without fear. I could never share my heart with him or ask him for a response. He never taught me with kindness. All that I ever received from my father were accusations, threats and insults. That's what 'father' meant to me. 'Maybe that's what you're like too?' I hurled at God. 'How could I ever call you "Father?" If you are really my Father, let me tell you what I'm feeling and thinking! I could never do that with the other father you gave to me! Where were you when I needed you, when I was alone and there was no one to defend me? Where were you when those unspeakably horrible things happened to me? What kind of father are you anyway? I don't need that kind of do-nothing father. I don't even want you! Jesus is enough for me; he's all I want! I don't care what you're thinking of doing with me now! I don't feel close to you at all!' The build-up within me of many years of pain, hurt and bitterness burst like a ruptured dam that afternoon.

Following this outburst of 'disgraceful' behaviour, I thought that thunder would boom from heaven and lightning strike me down. Instead – to my utter amazement – I heard a quiet, tender Voice. 'I want to give you everything that you were deprived of for all those years. I want to pamper you.'

It was so unexpected that I stopped dead in my tracks. My heart filled with indescribable joy. I began to grasp that I could actually tell my heavenly Father everything that I was thinking about. He wouldn't explode in anger at me; he wouldn't judge me; he wouldn't rush to punish me. For the first time in my life I knew what it felt like when a father loves you and accepts you totally. I experienced feelings of trust and security I had never known. I walked home that day with a joyful heart, my head held high like a child confident in her father and certain of his love. The words to a song kept going over and over inside my mind and heart. 'My Father loves me! My Father loves me! My Father loves me!' I wanted to shout to everyone around me.

Later that same day I was called to the office of the senior pastor of our church. I went with great reluctance, with puffy cheeks and red, tear-stained eyes. Why did I have to go at this inopportune moment? To my utter astonishment, the pastor handed me an envelope with 1,000 rand in it (approximately £80 at that time). 'Use this for whatever personal needs you have,' he said. He also told me he didn't usually do things like this, but the Holy Spirit had impelled him. He was to tell me, 'This is a gift of love to you from your heavenly Father.'

The next day my friend Melisha came to see me. God had spoken to her. 'He wants to pamper you.' The Lord directed her to take me to a store with the invitation to buy anything that I wanted. In the days following a lot of similar incidents occurred. None of these people had any external knowledge of what had taken place within me. It was simply God, who fulfils his word. In all these ways, he generously poured out on me his incomparable love and mercy.

What a God! I love him so much! He is forever alive. He is mighty. And he is not put off by our weakness. He alone has the power to take our weaknesses and problems and help us grow strong in his Spirit. My respect and reverence for him and my living relationship with him grew and expanded following this honest time of deep processing. Instead of a 'proper religious form' I now had a wide-open, real and profoundly trusting relationship.

In this closeness to my heavenly Father I felt secure, loved and cared for in the depths of my soul. I had never known anything like this with my earthly father. Instead of waking each morning with a feeling of hopelessness, loneliness and dull despair, now I awoke to joy and lightness of heart. It was so amazing that, at first, I could hardly believe it. Later I came to realize that this joy in spirit came from knowing that God my heavenly Father loved me so much.

> Be merciful, just as your Father is merciful.
>
> Luke 6:36

Whenever I did something he didn't like, my earthly father would threaten to kill me or bury me alive. If he considered me guilty of something, his rage would fall upon me even though he himself did many wrong things. Every sinful person lives in this kind of paradoxical judgment, doing the same things that they harshly judge others for. The Bible clearly states:

> You, therefore, have no excuse, you who pass judgment on someone else, for at whatever point you judge another, you are condemning yourself, because you who pass judgment do the same things.
>
> Romans 2:1

My father was no exception in this. But when I was wrong and guilty of many things, God revealed himself to me through Jesus Christ – the holy and spotless Lamb – who died in my place. He did this in love to save me from my wickedness. What a wonderful healing and comfort to know that you have this kind of God, a true Father, mighty and holy, who loved you, loves you, and will love you forever, just as you are.

I never felt accepted by my earthly father, or by many others around me. He constantly rebuked, criticized and accused me. The hurt went so deep that I couldn't accept myself. Throughout my childhood and youth there were those who were kind and good to me. Even though I was the daughter of a well-known drunkard and suffered the humiliation and sadness of that, these friends were rays of warm sunshine in the midst of the frozen winter of my life. They brought beauty into my world and warmth into my heart, enabling me to retain hope and not go permanently stone cold.

But the role of immediate family and especially of one's own father is huge in the formation of self-identity and response to the world, and I was enormously wounded by mine. When I was reconciled with my heavenly Father through the sacrifice of Christ, he taught me to love my earthly father exactly as he is, regardless of anything.

As part of the healing process, I wrote a letter to my father, pouring out the pain of my wounded soul. 'You were the one appointed by God to protect me,' I raged. 'But you left so much pain and wounding in my soul.' I confessed that there were times I hated him with every fibre of my being. But now I understood how much he must have been suffering himself, 'like a small lad terribly in need of true love.' He had not been loved any more than I was. I told him how I had considered suicide and confessed my complicity in the murder of his unborn grandchild.

I blamed my sin on my father's lack of love until I met the Eternal One, who was able to heal, set free and restore everything that was damaged in my life. In my letter, I shared the gospel with my father and my hope that his life, too, would be transformed by Jesus.

'Now, thanks to the Lord, I love you very much,' I confessed. 'I thank him that he opened my eyes, and I am thankful that you are my earthly father. This has been the will of God, both for you and for me.'

This letter was never sent. It was more for God and for myself than for my father, so that I could honestly express my feelings and work through a healing process with the Lord's help.

More than once I have met struggling people who, with the mention of the word 'father', immediately lose all joy and peace. It seemed they were ready to forgive in Christ anyone that they needed to, for anything at all, except their own father. What a tragedy! If that is true of you, believe me – there is one who is able to heal all of your wounds and give you peace in your heart, deep comfort and even joy. He is alive!

> Come to me, all you who are weary and burdened, and I will give you rest. Take my yoke upon you and learn from me, for I am gentle and humble in heart, and you will find rest for your souls. For my yoke is easy and my burden is light.
>
> Matthew 11:28–30

Now, with the Lord's gracious healing, I know clearly that my father loved me as he was able, but was never really capable of expressing that love. I remembered when he protected me against my brother-in-law's plot to have me murdered. From that time my relationship with my father began to improve, but the great change only took place after I came to Christ. His gracious work of sanctification, with its healing and cleansing inside my soul, started to grow a sturdy sprout of genuine honour and respect for my father. Previously I looked at him through the eyes of a frightened little girl, and all I could see was wounding thorns. But when we begin to look at people through eyes healed by God's love, everything changes. Only then are we able to see into the beautiful, suffering soul, which has been hidden behind the thorny, frightening exterior.

I was finally able to write, and send, another letter to my father from a completely healed and genuine heart, full of regret for my terrible attitude towards him and expressing my love and gratitude. This was thanks to a miracle that God worked in my heart and mind; and God gave me opportunities to share the gospel with my father face to face for a while. My heavenly Father taught me how to love my earthly father, and I am so thankful.

Part Four

Less of Self – Fully Alive

Arise, shine, for your light has come,
   and the glory of the LORD rises upon you.
See, darkness covers the earth
   and thick darkness is over the peoples,
but the LORD rises upon you
   and his glory appears over you.
Nations will come to your light,
   and kings to the brightness of your dawn.
                                    Isaiah 60:1–3

11

Married Love

One day soon after my conversion to Christ, I was seeking to convey to my older sister the joy of my connection to this loving Saviour. She responded, 'Well, if your God is so good, why doesn't he give you a good husband?'

I answered, 'If he wants to, he will give me such a husband, but even if he doesn't, I will serve him with all my heart because he has done so much for me.' In the end, God in his great grace and mercy did give me a wonderful husband and two awesome children. But for this to happen in God's way, it was crucial for me to first give up all my rights and entirely entrust myself to his best will. When we allow God to give us what he wants to, what he gives will be the very best.

The first time I met my future husband was in 2006. I had returned to my homeland from South Africa for a few weeks during a break in my Bible school studies. At the time I was engaged to John. We had agreed to seek the Lord and test our relationship during this time apart. During these weeks I was asked to speak several times at my home church in southern Russia. Following one of those messages, a fine-looking man came up to me at the front of the church, thanked me for my message and gave me a small gift.

I had never seen him before. Nothing notable happened in our conversation. Later I discovered that he had started coming to the church recently. Two years earlier he had tragically lost his wife in a car accident, leaving him with two small children. At that moment I could have never guessed that two and half years later, I would become the wife of this young man.

Back in South Africa my engagement to John ended, leading to a God-ordained time of deep divine dealing and healing in my soul, as I have explained. In January 2007 I returned to Russia, to my home church in Temer-Kala. After all of God's inner working in my life, I had entered a time of peace and freedom. I was happy to fully devote myself to the work of the Lord. If the subject of marriage came up, it caused no disquiet in me, so profound was the peace I now knew. If someone tactlessly asked, 'Why don't you get married?' even that did not upset me as it had in earlier years.

I gave myself to various areas of Christian ministry: seminars, preaching and teaching, prayer ministries, home meetings, counselling and outreach to the sick and the poor. My soul was satisfied because this was where my heart was. From the beginning of my Christian life, I longed for the love of God to flow through me to others in every way. I didn't even care about being paid.

Inevitably in our eastern culture I encountered significant difficulties as an unmarried woman involved in ministry. Two cultural factors stood against me. First, I was an unmarried woman in leadership. The other was simply that I was a woman. In many churches in my home region, limiting stereotypes existed regarding the role of women in ministry. In prayer, I concluded that given the strength of my calling, the Lord was probably leading me to be married, both for peace and well-being in my life and for effectiveness in Christian ministry.

I still longed for a life partner and to raise a family together with my husband. The Creator himself planted this desire from the beginning of creation, and thus it is a holy and lawful right and desire of every human being. Of course, there are those who are led to give up that right to more totally fulfil their specific divine calling. The Bible respects and honours those who are called to serve the Lord on the path of singleness. In the final analysis, it all depends on God's will and his plan for each of us.

My precious aunt-in-the-Lord, Zina, had always dreamed of finding me a husband. When I shared with her my prayerfully concluded sense of direction, she rejoiced exuberantly! Along with another sister, she started to regularly fast and pray for my future marriage. I had been through a lot in this area of my life, and I did not want to make more unwise mistakes. The clear leading of the Lord, his strong confirmation, was what I was after.

About two months later, I started spending time with Erbulat, the man whom I had first met at the front of the church in 2006. Erbulat worked at the same place as my dear friend Hadizhat, as an office manager in a business run by our pastor. We had a lot of common interests and enjoyed being together, but it was just a friendship. As I understood it, he was in another relationship. I didn't discover until later that Erbulat's dating relationship with the other woman had already ended.

In the following month, a Christian leader from South Africa and I led a week-long seminar on inner healing at our home church. Erbulat was asked to head up transportation and security needs for the seminar; this meant extended time together each day. Only on a friendship basis, of course. However, almost immediately after my colleague returned to South Africa, Erbulat initiated an unexpected conversation with me.

He was direct and to the point about his interest in a serious romantic relationship.

I discovered some time later that this conversation was not without the strong impetus of my praying Aunt Zina! A short, but highly influential, conversation with her had encouraged him to share his heart with me boldly.

When Erbulat and I began to talk about God's will for our relationship, we soon decided that we needed to give ourselves to serious fasting and prayer. It was very important to have confirmation from God that he was bringing us together, and if he was, to consecrate our future marriage to the Lord. Before any decision about possible engagement, we decided to enter into a three-week fast, drinking only water.

This was extremely difficult for me, but Erbulat said, 'There is spiritual power in such a decision. God has given us the freedom to choose. When we make a choice here on earth to seek after his will, power is exercised in the spiritual world.' Following these words, I was flooded with courage, and we trusted ourselves into God's hands.

From the second to the ninth day of this fast, I suffered attacks of excruciating pain throughout my bones and muscles. Words can't describe how difficult it was! But my decision remained firm, and I gave no consideration to stopping. The eighth day of the fast was the wedding of two of our close friends. We could not *not* go to this wedding and *not* join in the congratulations to these dear friends. The tables were loaded with scrumptious food for the celebration, but with the help of the Lord, we resisted the fierce temptation and peacefully passed the test.

This fast was intense for me, but the desire to please God and know his will was even more intense. On the ninth day I felt extremely weak. When I got on my feet, I could barely put one foot in front of the other. Even the sight of unappetizing fish at the fishmonger's stand started the saliva flowing.

Erbulat invited me to go for a walk along the sea. During this walk, I felt faint and even somewhat fearful. Maybe I should just drink some juice . . . We sat down, and here Erbulat amazed me. He was fasting for the first time in his life. I was the more experienced, having fasted many times previously.

Erbulat quietly said, 'That moment when the battle between the flesh and the spirit reaches its peak – that's the moment when you either fall back and lose something precious, or press through and gain a new position in God. If a person presses through to completion, there's victory, and you taste new depths in God's Spirit.'

There was great spiritual power in his words. I had the feeling that the whole spiritual world was watching to see what decision I would make. I would not give up – I was going forward to victory. At that moment I literally came alive; I felt a remarkable lightness of spirit. I was aware of feeling distinctly different than I had just minutes before. It was a moment of powerful spiritual breakthrough. The physical pain disappeared. In the days following, the fasting became very peaceful.

Only in the last two or three days of this three-week fast did I again experience strong pangs of hunger – so strong that I cried. Like no time previously, I began to intercede for all those in the world suffering from hunger. I understood at a deep level the awfulness of a death from starvation.

At the conclusion of this fast, not the slightest doubt remained in my soul that Erbulat was the man God had sent into my life to be my future husband. Our wedding took place three months later.

In contrast to our original plan to marry quietly among a small circle of friends, our wedding ended up being large and extravagant. The money which Erbulat and I personally possessed would not have been enough to host more than ten or twenty people, but we felt a strong leading of the Holy Spirit to organize a huge celebration and depend on the Lord for everything.

Our marriage was birthed in our local church. It was right to invite the entire church to our wedding. They were our spiritual family. One never thinks of which family members to invite or not invite to such a crucial celebration. It's the same in one's spiritual family. After all, aren't we brothers and sisters? Our local church at that time was around 250 people. And we told everyone, 'Not only are you invited, but please bring your unsaved friends.'

Of course, all Erbulat's relatives and all my relatives were also invited. When we put together our church family, our own extended families, and other circles of friends, we realized we needed a very large wedding venue. Instead of the small, inexpensive facility we had at first envisioned, we ended up reserving one of the largest event centres in the city.

Earlier as we prayed about our wedding, the thought flashed into my mind that we should hold the ceremony in the reception hall during the banquet. This was a shockingly innovative idea. In our eastern Muslim culture in the north Caucasus region, the actual wedding covenant is performed separately by the mullah before the public reception with its banquet food, dancing and speeches. Even Christian weddings in this region are performed briefly in a home or church building, followed by the reception.

I prayed that if this idea was from God, he would give strong help to bring it about. As we approached the time for the wedding covenant and the reception, it became apparent that there was not enough space in our small church building for this large group of people to witness the covenant. The choice presented itself – either move the wedding ceremony to a different date and location, or hold the Christian wedding right in the midst of the wedding banquet celebration.

But what about my staunch Muslim relatives? They had all agreed to come to the wedding celebration. What would happen when they discovered that we were conducting a Christian ceremony at the same time, at the same location, in their presence? It had the potential to become unpleasant or even explosive. On the other hand, it had become evident that it was God's will to go forward in this manner. Of course, in any situation, God's will is the deciding factor.

When you put all your trust in the Lord and in following his will, you're never put to shame.

> I sought the Lord, and he answered me;
>> he delivered me from all my fears.
> Those who look to him are radiant;
>> their faces are never covered with shame.
>
> Psalm 34:4,5

More than 350 friends and relatives gathered. Several of my precious relatives glowered angrily when the Christian wedding ceremony began, but God covered them with his love, light and joy. There was no disturbance. The wedding far exceeded my hopes and dreams. Even my past Muslim friends came to the wedding – some of the most famous musicians and singers in our region. When I invited them, I was not at all sure that any of them would come. Not only did they come, but they blessed the wedding with their musical talents and then blessed my husband and me with generous gifts. I was amazed and deeply moved by their response.

Our wedding videographer, who had covered many weddings, told us that this was the most joyful, beautiful and thrilling wedding that he had ever participated in. Furthermore, he had never seen so many 'superstars' at one wedding. God gave us the most talented chef in our city to prepare the food, and it was exquisite. God even gave us a limousine! We had never considered such an expense, but one of our friends surprised us with the gift, and so we came and went in style.

There was no alcohol at the festivities. Many of our non-Christian friends could not understand how there could be so much joy, laughter and exuberance – with no alcohol! The wedding turned into a celebration of God's love in a big circle of God's redeemed family. Its effect was a living sermon and testimony of the Lord's power, love, joy and hope to many unredeemed people.

Later a Christian sister told me about an unbelieving friend whom she had invited. Towards the end of the wedding this friend began to sob uncontrollably. My Christian sister asked if something was wrong. Through overflowing tears, the friend said that she had always dreamed about the kind of joy and freedom that she had seen here at this wedding, but until that night she had thought it was an unreachable fantasy.

As regards finances, we not only didn't have to ask for help or take out a loan, there was money left over – more than enough for a beautiful honeymoon trip. However, one of our Christian brothers was in huge need right at that moment. We decided with joy to give the money to him and have never worried about the honeymoon or suffered in the least. Our treasure is in heaven.

At first my father had rejoiced at my marriage and at getting to know my new husband. All was well up to and at the time of the wedding. But when we travelled to visit my father a short time afterwards, his emotional state had changed. He was beside himself with rage and threw my husband and me out of the house. This was accompanied by threats against us of the most violent nature. In the intervening weeks some influential religious rabble-rousers had done their dark work in my father's life. And all this arose from the fact that my husband and I had not been afraid to openly speak about our lives and our love for Jesus Christ at our wedding. We had no regrets. It is impossible to please both unredeemed people and a holy God, and each person in the end chooses whom he will please.

Following this amazing wedding, I became simultaneously the wife of a wonderful man and the mother of two children, Amina, born in 1997, and Manop, born in 1994. When we began our family life together, I began to understand how far I still was from holiness. I had often given teachings about how to be an excellent wife, how to properly raise children, about how to be a wholehearted Christian. I had become a hero of the faith to many. But now, I entered into a time of seeing my own genuine condition at a much deeper level when engaged in interactive family life. God was bringing me into a time of intensified humility, purification, and dying to my sinful nature.

After the death of their mother, in 2004, the children had lived with Erbulat's mother. So they had lived with her for more than four years at the time of our marriage. It didn't seem that anyone was paying too much attention to their upbringing.

'They're just growing up like wild weeds,' a neighbour told me when I first visited Erbulat's parents. It was a gift of God that Erbulat's mother was willing to sacrificially take the children in and feed and clothe them when she was elderly herself and not in good health.

The situation was complicated because both sets of grandparents had a very distorted view of Erbulat and myself due to our Christian faith. There was a lot of opposition, disturbance and unjust criticism directed at us, and they sought to prevent the children from living with us. We steadfastly refused to take offence. These dear folks didn't know God's Word or the Holy Spirit. Much patience was called for.

Erbulat's parents were much more receptive towards us. The mother of Erbulat's first wife, however, was extremely antagonistic. She sought to agitate the family against us, constantly declaring that we were part of a cult. She attacked us to the children themselves, saying, 'You don't need to have anything to do with your dad.' She called us 'fanatics' and insisted it would be dangerous for the children to become too religious. This grandmother believed a person should be restrained about faith matters, and live at a nominal level like everyone else. She possessed an extremely sharp tongue to go along with her suspicious, antagonistic outlook. It was a diabolical combination. At moments of indignation and outrage, insulting phrases flew from her mouth like poisoned arrows whose wounds went deep. I'm not exaggerating to say she terrorized both us and the children.

The absurd allegations and slander flowed especially towards me. This woman tested my level of spirituality, patience and unconditional love to the extreme. I can't claim that I always passed the test with high marks. But the Holy Spirit was truly helping me to triumph over my negative emotions, and to seek a path of peace. For my husband and me, efforts to preserve family peace often called for unbelievable strength. To peacefully talk with her about the importance of family and of a father in children's lives, was almost impossible. Praise to the Most High for this precious woman and all that we learned through this difficult travail! There isn't anything on this earth that cannot be triumphed over through the power of love.

I was adamant that the children needed to come to live with us. It is crucial for children to be raised in a family, especially with their God-given father and mother. The parents carry divine responsibility in forming the personality and character of the children as they grow. 'The sooner they can come to live with us, the better!' we said. It would not be easy. Much had already been lost and more had been sown into their lives in ungodly ways. Nonetheless, we saw potential for success and blessing to come with God's help.

'God gave me children prepared in advance,' I said, and sincerely rejoiced in this. Only the Lord can give children, and he gives them as he chooses, and to whom he chooses.

In the flesh, it would have been simpler to just live with my husband and together serve the Lord in Christian ministry. 'What are you thinking, Shaadia?' some people said – even fellow believers. 'This is a huge responsibility – they are not even your own children! Why, you have a ministry calling! You should just serve the Lord and not try to add this.' The prospect was enticing. Why take on additional burdens?

I understood early on that the Lord wanted to not only give me a husband, and Erbulat a wife, but to give these two precious children a family. At the time of our marriage, in August 2008, Amina was eleven and Manop was thirteen. I considered them as gifts from God, even while understanding that the calling in front of me was not easy. But what does it mean to serve the Lord? At first, my sense of calling went through a period of swirling confusion. What should I focus on? God calls us not to seek the most comfortable approach to life, but to be salt and light in a difficult world. That call is, first of all, to our own children in their challenging growth processes. Maybe these children, right now, were my primary calling.

In the first year of our marriage, we succeeded in bringing Amina to live with us. Her older brother, Manop, was only with us on school breaks and holidays. In general Amina was happy that her father had married and that she had a new home with a mother. At the same time she was extremely stubborn and headstrong, easily offended and rebellious. When she arrived, she seemed not to bring any sense of respect towards elders or obedience towards father and mother. Rather, her approach was to control everything.

Mixed with this was her thirst for love, a thirst so strong that it felt like the suction of a vacuum cleaner on my soul. A child who wanted to be loved, but did almost everything to make it difficult to love her. What a challenge! Honestly, sometimes I was beside myself with exhaustion and despair. I had spoken and taught about God's plan for us to love with his unconditional love, and now I faced what felt like the ultimate test. I can't boast about how I did – sometimes such anger rose within me at her behaviour. Not only did I experience a shortfall of love, I'm ashamed to admit that at times I hated her. True enough, these were only emotions. I would cry out in prayer, 'Lord, I hate her! I beg you, help me!' And the raw emotions would pass. It felt like I was being pressed through a meat grinder. Sometimes I lost it and screamed at Amina: 'Why am I being punished like this?' How many times I sobbed, humbled myself and repented to God – asking for his forgiveness and grace.

It's difficult even now to talk about these struggles. In the midst of all this, as I experienced his mercy, forgiveness, love and patience, God did a precious work of reality in my soul. The Lord was stripping away every external religious facade and any remnant of super-spirituality, and showing me my real condition underneath. He showed me the absolute weakness of my flesh.

'I am totally bankrupt and desperately in need of your holy grace,' I prayed. 'Only in this is there any hope for me!'

In this bare condition, I let his gracious Spirit saturate my being.

This may have been the most important step of all in the transformation of my life in Christ. At this depth, he was able to get a hold of my heart the way he needed to. He wanted my heart to be humble, patient, understanding, compassionate to others' weaknesses, thankful, gracious and capable of forgiving everything and loving unconditionally. Young Amina needed this too. As it happened in me, it began in her also. Victories started to come. Some days you could see love winning, encouraging, making things new in this young girl's life. And God was patiently, tenderly teaching me, strengthening me in his love.

The more I understood my utter weakness, the more gentle and patient I became. Just in time he helped me come to my senses. The Lord told me that children need to learn that parents are also imperfect people. If those parents are open to the Lord, the children can learn as they see their parents grow. The children can even learn to forgive their parents' shortcomings (just as the parents forgive the children), while continuing to honour and respect their parents. If they can learn to forgive their parents, it will serve as spiritual protection in their lives – finding peace and resolution not only for the human shortcomings of parents, but also for when they step out into the wider world, meeting people and forming relationships in the future.

I am so thankful that the Lord sent me such a wonderful daughter! Amina is a courageous girl, and the Lord accomplished a great work in my life through her. The intensity of family life gives a person a powerful opportunity for deeper humility and sanctification if they will embrace it. Thank you,

Amina, for your part in helping me know God better and be conformed more to the likeness of Christ.

Amina ferociously thirsted for love, like a fish on dry land craves for the water. But she wasn't capable of earning it; usually, just the opposite. What a familiar picture! Each one of us is in exactly the same position regarding the love of God. None of us deserve love; we're not able to earn it, even though it's what we long for more than anything else. But the Lord loved us first, sacrificially and unconditionally.

> This is love: not that we loved God, but that he loved us and sent his Son as an atoning sacrifice for our sins.
>
> 1 John 4:10

> But God demonstrates his own love for us in this: while we were still sinners, Christ died for us.
>
> Romans 5:8

Once, Amina revealed to me that she had feared I would send her back to her grandmother. Thanks be to God, even in my most desperate moments I never had that thought. She was not to blame for the fact that no one had given attention to her upbringing. This bright and good-hearted girl had experienced truckloads of difficulty in her short existence. These had left their mark on her character and habits. I could never have allowed Amina to go through one more rejection! That would be to deny Christ myself. Erbulat and I had already shared so much with Amina. We prayed together almost every day, and I was absolutely determined not to give up.

We worked at training Amina in character and self-discipline.

'People look at you and think you're an angel,' I told Amina one day. 'They look at me as if I'm a saint. But you and I both know what the reality is. And God knows. So let's both work on ourselves.'

By this point she was able to understand the spiritual battle we both faced.

We worked and worked. There was tenderness and fierceness, encouragement and punishment, prayer and conversation, and of course, lots of tears and hugs – which she needed most of all. During this time, Amina changed amazingly, but I changed no less than she. The joy of victory exceeded all difficulties that we had faced together. We refused to give up and together received a huge reward. If I had not known Christ, success like this would not have been possible, so I give all thanks and praise to him! Amina became a huge blessing in our work for the Lord. Many opportunities for acquaintance and fellowship with local people came about through her!

12

Love Reaches Out

Eight months after our wedding, the Lord called us to leave Temer-Kala and go as missionaries to Dahunsk, a smaller city in the mountains. This city had always been in a special category of difficulty, but we knew we were called, and we said yes.

The thought of Dahunsk had always evoked dread in me. I prayed for its inhabitants, but never believed that the Lord would send me there. There was no Christian presence in this city or nearby. In the past a small Christian chapel had stood in this town, but it had long ago been burned down.

My grandfather, a Muslim holy man, was buried in Dahunsk. A mosque had been constructed at the site of his grave, and fervent Muslims went to this location to worship Allah. Approximately fifteen years before we moved to Dahunsk, a husband and wife – evangelical Christians – had gone to serve the Lord there. They had been tortured and burned to death in the city square in the middle of the day, accused of stealing children to sell their internal organs. From that time no Christians had arisen with the readiness or calling to serve the Lord in this city.

When we understood that the Lord was calling us to Dahunsk, my attitude towards the city drastically changed. Some of our Christian brothers and sisters said that we must be out of our minds, but I wanted to get there as soon as possible.

We hoped to find a one-family home to rent. Nothing felt right, but then we found a two-room apartment. It was not very big, and those two adjoining rooms were very much in need of repair. An elderly woman – the owner – lived in the other two rooms of the house. There was a shared veranda. It was totally illogical, but in our spirits we knew this was the right place. Trusting in the Lord, we made an agreement with the landlady and in less than a week moved into these rooms.

I remember the tiredness I felt after our arrival. I sat on a pile of things that had been unloaded from a van. The gloomy light revealed peeling plaster. A chilly draft hit me from all sides. Looking around, I didn't know where to start. Out of my feelings of helplessness I started to cry. 'Lord, look at this! How the wicked prosper who don't even want to hear about you! And we, who are willing to go to the end of the earth for you, live in these conditions – and our children also! – while we seek to do your work. Is this all that you can share with us? Is this really what you want for your children? I am terribly tired, weak, and I don't understand anything. Help me! Say something to me, please.'

Once again our precious Lord did not delay in speaking wisdom and encouragement. Immediately the Holy Spirit spoke to my heart. 'My kingdom is not of this world. Many seek material blessings; but I am seeking those who will follow me.' A minute or two later my husband came into the room with similar words of truth and encouragement. It was enough. Shortly after, I found myself revived, joyfully and energetically putting my hand to the tasks of our new home.

How many times it's been confirmed that God sent me the husband who was exactly right for me! It was amazing when my mother, who still considers herself a Muslim, expressed to me with sincere feeling that Erbulat was a godly man. She's never been able to fully relate to Erbulat due to the language barrier between them – Erbulat is from the Nagay ethnic group – but she saw in him the light of God; the quiet testimony of God's love, shown through actions of love.

When we first travelled to Dahunsk, we felt in our spirits the heavy spiritual opposition. Even before we moved in, we were robbed. That had never happened to us anywhere else. We remained in God's peace and had no intention of shrinking back, but we were keenly aware of the reality of oppressive strongholds.

A few days after we moved in, I woke up suddenly in the middle of the night to a powerful feeling of uneasiness verging on horror. A type of curtain opened in front of me, and I saw hideous beings filling the air space above me. They seemed to have entered through the walls and the doors and were preparing to consume us. This was so real that my hair stood on end from terror. I started to pray, but the oppression was so heavy that I knew I couldn't deal with this alone.

I woke Erbulat. He didn't see anything, but immediately felt that we were not alone in the room. He sensed a heavy, oppressive cloud of evil. We fervently prayed in agreement for about half an hour. Finally things calmed down, and peace was restored to our hearts. Similar oppressive attacks happened more than once in the months ahead.

Another night I woke, gazing down on myself from above. On the bed, I looked like a corpse. It seemed like some kind of vile crime was underway, being perpetrated by a murderous spirit. I wanted to cry out, but I couldn't make a sound. Right then, my husband awoke and shook me. Instantly everything stopped. I was so thankful to the Lord that he woke Erbulat to help me, even though my husband didn't know what was going on. I told him what I had been experiencing, and we prayed in agreement and peacefully fell back to sleep.

Soon after this, I began getting thoughts about death. Some days I consciously said out loud, 'I think I will die soon.' Related to this were occasional feelings of total apathy or hopelessness about everything, or a sense of the uselessness of our mission work.

'I really should just die.' This thought regularly visited me over a period of about two months. Erbulat and I stood against the enemy, fasted, prayed and worked with all our hearts in our field of calling. Praise the Lord for my husband! His words of encouragement and wisdom were incredibly strengthening. But serious warfare had begun, and we needed additional support.

I feel deep thankfulness to the Lord for the brothers whom he sent. Two missionary servants of the Lord from Switzerland came to see us at this time. They had a great deal of experience in Christian ministry in unreached locations where the strongholds were immense. They understood exactly what was going on. These two were uniquely equipped to discern the spiritual realities, effectively serve us and greatly encourage us.

The older of the two was especially gifted in prophetic insight. While praying, the Lord showed him the spiritual condition of this region where we lived and served. 'I was overwhelmed by what I saw,' he told us. 'This is the city of Satan! You need constant powerful spiritual support!'

After they ministered to us, and with some extended times of prayer, at last I felt free. Again I desired to live. It was like being raised from the dead. What a blessing this freedom and alive-ness was!

Spiritual warfare is real, and the devil prowls around like a roaring lion seeking whom he can devour (see 1 Peter 5:8), using whatever hook he can get a hold of. But the Lord has defeated all the power of the enemy, and God will never leave us or forsake us. This is why we need brothers and sisters in the body of the Lord. His power is multiplied when we function together.

Thinking back, I am grateful for all the foundations laid in my life before we embarked on this missionary obedience. Every ounce of it was important for the calling to that city. First of all, the heart desire to serve him in a place completely unreached was undoubtedly planted in me by the Lord himself. Without that vision, we couldn't have endured the intense spiritual battles associated with this calling. Furthermore, after arriving in the city, I came to the conclusion that we might be called to a labour in which we would not see the fruit during our lifetime, but we were to give ourselves to this labour with all our hearts.

When we left on this missionary venture to this unreached province, I was still somewhat under the influence of a widely circulating 'prosperity gospel'. This prosperity doctrine asserted there would always be huge church fellowships with expensive buildings – accompanied by quick revivals, instant miracles and mass conversions. I was not lacking experiences of Holy Spirit power, but this particular false representation of Jesus' work in an evil, fallen world gradually collapsed within me like a house of cards. It was replaced by reality.

> I have told you these things, so that in me you may have peace. In this world you will have trouble. But take heart! I have overcome the world.
>
> John 16:33

'Are you ready to serve me, even if you never personally see the fruit of your labours on this earth? If you sow for others to harvest?' This question rang loudly inside my being about two months after our arrival in the region. My heart responded with complete peace. My mind understood that this was the nature of faithfulness in a fallen world. Following further times of prayer and study, I understood that our calling was to abide in the Vine. This was the only way that fruit would come. Our calling was to be his representatives, follow Jesus day by day, carry our cross, and let his light shine through us. Following this path, good fruit would inevitably follow – *his* fruit – and it was not for me to worry about quantities. That was in his hands. Whether I saw great results on this earth was not my concern. Faithfulness to what he called me to do – that was my only consideration.

As this reality settled into my being, I began to approach my service to the Lord in a new way. Earlier I used to fret that I was 'wasting' so much energy on mundane household matters. Now I saw that I could serve God daily in everything. There was no division between 'spiritual' activities and 'other' activities – everything was spiritual. Finally, genuine Christianity permeated all of my life. I found great joy in letting the light of Christ shine through me, wherever I was and whatever I was about.

> In the same way, let your light shine before others, that they may see your good deeds and glorify your Father in heaven.
>
> Matthew 5:16

Amina was in the seventh grade that year. When Christmas came, we organized a celebration with gifts and beautiful food for all Amina's classmates. Oh, how we prayed! First of all, we prayed that everyone would come. It was like a miracle, wonderful and amazing. All twenty students from her class came! At first they were shy and cautious. They were not accustomed to all being invited to the home of one of the girls. We prepared a special programme for the party. To our joy, some of our believing friends from Temer-Kala came to help. The atmosphere was festive and casual, and the guests began to relax and have fun. In this happy atmosphere, we were able to tell about this Christmas holiday and why we celebrated it. It was comfortable to talk about the miracle of Jesus Christ coming into the world. We believers were aware of the powerful presence of the Holy Spirit among us.

The children happily played games, ate and listened to our stories with great interest. A number of local adults also came, and they even joyfully welcomed our prayers for them. We had prepared gifts of sweets and Christmas CDs with stories and videos about God's love and his wonderful plan for each of us. The evening was so much fun that none of the children wanted to leave.

The next afternoon, with some trepidation, I waited for Amina to come home from school. What would the reaction to our Christmas party be? Although I had deep peace in the Lord, it was still possible there'd be a severe reaction in this culture. I needed to be prepared for anything. Obedience to God doesn't mean that everything will necessarily go smoothly in this world.

Amina came home from school. On the doorstep she exclaimed, 'They're even friendlier than they were before – they're treating me like I'm somebody really special!'

Oh, what relief and joy I felt. Several of the girls in her class even began to confess to her that they realized they were sinful, and that now they understood there was a path of forgiveness and salvation available to them. Praise to the Lord! His mercy and power are great! We were able to go forward serving the Lord peacefully.

There's nothing exotic about real missionary work in unreached places. Once an acquaintance came to see us. He described with great fervency how beautiful and wonderful everything was in Turkey. He announced that he intended to go and live there as a missionary. I started feeling really sad – not for us, but for him: 'What's going on here? Why go to Turkey when there are large numbers of Christian servants already located there? Really, is missionary service a vehicle for living in an exotic location on someone else's tab? Who are you kidding?' Praise God, there are many who literally lay their lives down, quietly and humbly, on behalf of Christ in sacrificial service. That's what fires my vision and inspires my heart.

Our missionary life in this unreached, resistant territory began with no stable financial support. It was practically impossible for my husband to find work in this mountainous region. Indeed, many men from this area regularly leave to find work temporarily in other parts of Russia. Erbulat worked with his hands, helping people, usually as a kind gift, occasionally receiving a small amount of pay. His helping hands were part of our Christian service. We had an old car. More than once I needed to push it, so that the engine would turn over. That car travelled by our prayers. There was an outside tap in the garden behind our house, but the water was only turned on for a few hours once or twice a week. At those times we filled as many containers as possible. From this water we bathed and washed dishes and clothes. We heated water in a big pan on a hotplate. Water access was worse in the winter. Sometimes the outside tap froze entirely, and then we'd have to find a temporary new source. My resourceful husband, master of many trades, actually created some necessary furniture for us out of leftover boards.

Nevertheless, we rejoiced that by the grace of God we could live there! We loved the local people with a burning love and were ready to stay there for our whole lives, offering Jesus to this region. But it wasn't easy. Far from it. I personally struggled with the absence of other fellow workers.

> Then he said to his disciples, 'The harvest is plentiful but the workers are few. Ask the Lord of the harvest, therefore, to send out workers into his harvest field.'
>
> Matthew 9:37,38

We earnestly prayed. But no one else agreed to come to this region. It was necessary to take every step on our own. We prepared food and fed many people, giving ourselves to acts of service both physically and spiritually. And, of course, we had to keep up with our own household.

Several times really difficult moments arose, when I felt like I was wearing out – this feeling was intensified by physical health problems and pain. At times I was discouraged: 'No one is responding to our efforts. It's all meaningless.' If even the strongest sometimes feel weak, and generals give in to exhaustion, I guess it can happen to me too.

Once I was grieving so much and pouring out my helpless despair to the Lord; I cried, 'Lord, why are there so few who are ready to totally follow you? With what kind of eyes do people read the Bible, if they ignore the most important things? Why is there such a lack of understanding of missionary service? We're driving this broken-down car that needs me, as a woman, to get out and push it, while at the same time hundreds and thousands of Christians sit in big comfortable churches and drive their luxurious cars. We're scrimping every kopeck; living right on the edge. And there's so much work! The harvest potential in this place is truly plentiful, but everyone has their reason why they can't participate in this work. I long for even just one other person to join with us. It would so much lighten our load. Lord, I'm so tired. Forgive me! But it seems like everything we're doing is of no help to anyone, or even to you.' Tears coursed down my face.

At that moment I heard a still, small voice in my spirit. 'Shaadia, do not fear – I am your exceedingly great reward.' I was filled with amazement. Genuine joy penetrated my soul. I was feeling so weak that I absolutely didn't expect to hear words of support from the Lord. But this word carried nourishment and gave me unusual strength and courage. It was more than enough. 'He is with me. He is my reward. What could be better than that?'

God did answer our prayer for help. In the course of time we became acquainted with one local family who were believers in Jesus. The father had come to Christ while doing construction work in another part of Russia to earn money for his family. His joy knew no bounds when he discovered that we, followers of Jesus, had come here to live and to serve. He had prayed for two years for the Lord to send someone. His wife also came to faith a little later. We had the privilege of baptizing Artur and Aishat. The four of us became extremely close. They served as our helpers and our first disciples. What a great blessing and encouragement Artur and Aishat were for us! Truly they were the beginning of the future workers for the harvest.

So commenced a time of remarkable blessing for this difficult region. We openly testified to our faith. Many people came to our home. We fed them, both physically and spiritually; we helped everyone in every way that we possibly could. And the doors were open to visit many people in their homes.

Then, I became seriously ill. Every bone in my body ached, especially my right leg, which I couldn't even straighten out. The big toe on my right foot was so painful and inflamed that it was impossible to wear a shoe on that foot. For two months I took pain relief tablets, hoping that this wasn't serious and would soon pass, with prayer. But when I discovered, in the course of a medical examination, that I was on the verge of developing a fatal disease with consequent painful suffering, I saw this world and my life with completely new eyes.

Eighteen months earlier, two sisters in Christ with whom I had been very close died within a few weeks of each other. Both suffered greatly, one dying virtually in my arms. I had heard stories of how believers die with smiles on their faces, but that was not the case with these dear ones. I saw suffering and fear on their faces, and not the joy and tranquillity I had expected. This was very disappointing and upsetting to me. Everything I believed came under severe scrutiny and testing.

What is death like for God's children? Am I ready to be face-to-face with death personally? These questions took centre stage in my mind and spirit for long months after the deaths of my friends. Despite my years in the church, religious phrases seemed superficial. We must all face death personally; no one else can face it for you when that day comes. My mind could quote many passages in the Bible on this theme, but my heart was in total turmoil. Head knowledge wasn't helping me much. Only heart knowledge produces life.

Now doctors had discovered a tumour on my ureter, with other complications. I faced death myself. Like never before I understood how this temporal world, with its bright and multicoloured dancing lights, is capable of lulling people straight to eternal death. The only way to true life in the midst of these illusory swirls is through Jesus. In those hours I plunged into an excruciating battle between this world of the flesh and the world of the spirit. It was terrible in its intensity.

Specifically, I had to choose whether or not to undergo a dangerous emergency operation, which the doctor was urging.

My husband immediately began a fast – to seek the Lord's wisdom on our behalf. In this time of fasting and prayer, we both sensed that the Lord was giving us a choice as to whether to go with the operation or to decline the operation and fully give my life into God's hands. It was a desperately difficult decision for us. Did I fear death? I had never been face-to-face with death before in this way.

If I died (and it could come from either medical choice), it wouldn't even be a death for my faith in Christ! To simply die from an illness, in physical disarray, nothing of real significance having been accomplished for the kingdom of God . . . 'How does this all relate to my trust in God?' I wondered. 'Has my trust in God been conditional? What does it really mean, "do something significant for the kingdom of God"?'

I poured out my heart to God. 'Lord, life or death is really not that important. What is crucial is that I have the kind of trust in you that supersedes all my thinking, my understanding, my accountings, and my plans!' I came to see that the deepest issue was not death or life, but my unconditional trust relationship with my Lord.

In the face of all this, could I give my life fully into the hands of God with utter peace? Or would I cling to human life with every possible desperate physical contrivance? My struggle had nothing to do with whether medical efforts are good or not – many times they are used for good. In that critical moment, in that immediate situation, the question entirely focused on my personal trust in the faithfulness and eternal power and leading of the Lord. In the midst of that situation, we came to clarity that I should not have the operation – which meant that the doctors refused further treatment.

When we came to this clarity and announced our decision, I felt total surrender into the loving arms of God; it was as if the heavens opened above me. I felt amazingly free and joyful! Nothing held me any more in this earthly existence. Only then was I able to say 100 per cent to the Lord and to myself, 'I do not fear death! If you, Lord, want me to stay on this earth, then no illness or anything else will be an obstacle. If my earthly time has concluded, you are welcome to take me any time.'

This verse from the Bible became very precious to me in those days:

> I eagerly expect and hope that . . . now as always Christ will be exalted in my body, whether by life or by death. For to me, to live is Christ and to die is gain.
>
> Philippians 1:20,21

At this point I truly began to taste in reality what it meant to rest in the Lord. It became so simple – all I was to do was live in full surrender to him, walk with him day by day, and seek to please him every day in big things and small. I could thank him for absolutely everything, rejoice and trust him with every moment of my life, praise him with every intake of breath and every exhaling breath, no matter what was happening or what situation I might experience. Unconditional peace.

I was filled with overflowing supernatural joy. The Lord had his most fruitful plan for my life. And when the time came, I could leave this world with joy. It wasn't really of significance any more by which path or outcome I left this earth, because what was of utmost significance was that I completely trusted him in everything. Besides, there in heaven with God it was incomparably better. My life was hidden in Jesus. He had died for me, and death now held no sting. I was free. Someday in the future, a day decided by my heavenly Father, I would simply transition to eternity leaving my mortal body like some kind of temporary tent. How wonderful it is to live in this kind of freedom, which only the victorious Jesus can give to a person.

The doctors were shocked when we declined the operation and the overall proposed plan. It was around the middle of October 2009 when I signed out of the hospital, having been there for ten days, and we went forward to continue serving the Lord in our call. In the weeks and months following, my physical condition rapidly improved – in opposition to the expectation of the doctors. Wonder of wonders, my foot was restored to health, and I started to walk normally again! All praise and honour only to the Eternal God, who is good and faithful forever!

However, for twenty months I suffered from bleeding and occasional terrible pain in my kidneys and urinary tract system. Still, I was peacefully believing that only the Lord was capable of properly healing me in the way that he knew was best.

Then, in the year 2011, after a particularly difficult stretch of intense pain and bleeding, in a prayer meeting God instantly and decisively brought internal healing. In June of that year I went to Moscow, taking our daughter with me, to get the first edition of my book in Russian from one of the publishing houses there. During our stay in Moscow, my bleeding increased. I went to one of the Moscow churches for a Sunday service, and they announced that the next day in the evening a healing service would take place, organized by a group of visiting ministers. At the same moment I heard in the spirit that I should go for this service and there I would be healed. I went there without any doubt in my heart, knowing that I would be healed. And so it happened. As soon as one of the women ministers prayed for me with the laying on of hands, I was instantly healed.

It was a supernatural restoration in my body, which took place to the glory of God. After that there was no more bleeding. All praise and honour to Christ, my Lord and Saviour, who paid an unimaginable price for this gracious healing.

13

The Test of Love

Erbulat's son, Manop, spent holidays with us, as I mentioned earlier, but in May of 2010 he joined our family permanently.

At the beginning of June my husband and I felt called to a forty-day fast. Through the prayers and spiritual wisdom of the brothers from Switzerland – who came to our region every year for a couple of weeks, and who had helped us so powerfully in our spiritual battles in that place – we received the definitive encouragement we needed to go ahead. By the grace of God we fulfilled this challenging step of intercession on behalf of the local people living in that region.

The plan was to abstain from food and only drink water with perhaps a glass or half-glass of juice daily. Previously such a long, total fast from food had seemed unreachable to me. Although I often fasted, the discipline was always physically difficult. But now the time had come for an intercessory labour for spiritual breakthroughs in the region where we served, and peace accompanied our commitment.

From early on in the fast, my primary prayers ran towards the purifying fire of the Holy Spirit. Yes, we regularly interceded for the people living around us and in surrounding people groups. We poured out our hearts to the Lord for them. But, in my prayers, I returned again and again to the same thing. My soul kept crying out to the Lord with the words of a Russian gospel song: 'Purify me, Lord, with the fire of the Holy Spirit; clean out everything that gets in your way.'

The first eight days of the fast were extremely tough, physically. I still suffered from bleeding and occasional terrible pain in my kidneys and urinary tract at that time. Medical indicators would have seemed to counsel against a forty-day fast. I craved food and was tormented with physical weakness, but fasting is much more than abstaining from food. Jesus is the complete Healer. Knowing this, I continued to be at peace despite my physical problems.

I felt the peace of putting myself – body and soul – totally in the hands of God. It was an expression of intentionally trusting everything to him. Only he is the Source of my life, of my joy, and of my hope. I resolved to peacefully trust in the one who had created my body and given me life. He knows all things, and when we submit to him and to his wisdom, we are not risking anything. It was a huge step of faith and trust between me and my Lord.

Almost as soon as we began this fast, another trial raised its head. Our previously gentle and friendly landlady suddenly seemed to change. She started carping at us about every little thing. She got agitated and exploded almost every day. We came to realize that there were spiritual reasons involved here. We resolved to not react to any of the provocations, but to intentionally seek the path of patience and love.

> For our struggle is not against flesh and blood, but against the rulers, against the authorities, against the powers of this dark world and against the spiritual forces of evil in the heavenly realms.
>
> Ephesians 6:12

It was hard, especially when she started to prepare delicious meals right under our noses. Those tempting smells surrounded us. I even experienced physical pain in my stomach. Normally she prepared her meals in the summer kitchen in the far corner of the courtyard. But during our fast she began preparing all of her food on the common veranda right behind our living room window. There was nowhere to hide from the omnipresent aromas. The only thing to do was make peace with the situation and love her anyway.

More than once she became indignant and said cruel things. Even though we had patiently explained about our fast and the spiritual reasons, she virtually exploded at us. 'Why aren't you eating? Why are you observing this fast, anyway?' Nonetheless, the Holy Spirit continued to strengthen us.

On the ninth day of the fast I experienced an amazing flow of energy. That whole day I worked tirelessly to clean up and cultivate our overgrown garden. I didn't know what to do with all my excess energy. After that the fast was markedly easier. I always had enough strength for everything. We worked a lot, not only spiritually but also physically, and didn't get tired. Erbulat and I felt physically stronger than we had before the fast. Of course, as the days went on, our precious landlady kept us thinking about hunger with her constant cooking smells coming in through our window. Her methods seemed to taunt us, but we rejoiced at this testing and thanked God that through it we could become even stronger in spirit.

God never seemed to give me ideal conditions when I fasted. Time after time I was led to fast in the midst of challenging circumstances. 'Oh, Lord, give me a peaceful place to observe fasting and prayer, a place where I can focus on you for several days and block out everything else in this world.' He never seemed to give me that. I fasted and prayed during times of intense studies. Or in a dormitory among a crowd of people. Or in a congested city. Or even at home where I needed to prepare meals for other people. Or while attending wedding feasts or holidays. Praise God! He freed me from an unreal view of spirituality. He taught me that Christianity is a way of life, right in the midst of life, not something that requires special religious surroundings. It's a continual walk with him and fellowship with him in his presence wherever I am and whatever I'm doing.

The most difficult period came after the thirtieth day of the fast. My husband and I both suffered severe hunger pangs, accompanied by physical weakness again. At the same time, I was experiencing the powerful presence of God. My heart was broken before him like never before. I literally wept and moaned before him, often having no words at all. Most of all, I tasted the overwhelming holiness of God and the hopeless sinfulness and degeneracy of my own heart more than at any time previously. I cried and cried and cried. But these were tears of worship and adoration before a radiant God, and tears of deep repentance and cleansing in me. He purified my heart as with a powerful cleansing solution. The more he purified, the more powerfully I was impacted by his holiness. The clearer the mirror became, the more penetratingly his holy light hit me and exposed my human imperfection and utter need of his loving grace. I bowed before him even more and cried, 'Oh, God, cleanse me with the fire of your Holy Spirit!' Words will not suffice to describe the inner dealings of this time.

As I came to the end of this forty-day fast, a lot had changed inside me. First of all, my relationship to my husband, to my children, and to my service to the Lord. Later my daughter said to me, 'You became so kind and wonderful after that fast! Before that you were good, but now you are so much better!'

On the last day of the fast I was deluged by the Holy Spirit. He showed me amazing heavenly things, beyond human description. I felt so healthy that it was as if I had never had a medical problem. I felt stronger and more vital – physically, emotionally and spiritually.

Fasting and prayer, in the name of Jesus and based on his Word, is a powerful spiritual weapon in the Lord (see 2 Corinthians 10:3,4). First of all, it transforms the person; secondly, through this spiritual power, many problems and illnesses are defeated. Finally, it brings down the powers of evil. That's why our fleshly nature, with all of its strong desires, fights against such hard fasting. But the way God works through our fasting and prayer will be beyond our finite human expectations.

After the completion of our fast, our landlady came to me with a gift. With tears in her eyes, she expressed her admiration to us about the amazing 'feat' we had accomplished. She was simply overwhelmed that my husband and I had fulfilled this long fast when she couldn't even abstain from food for a day. She spoke to us as if there had been no antagonism during the days of fasting. Praise to the Lord! Our victory is in him, and in all things we only need to walk in patience and trust towards him. In this path, without fail, there will always be a positive outcome.

Five days after the end of our fast, like thunder out of a clear sky, the phone rang. Our friends in the capital told us that our pastor and bishop, a spiritual father to us, had been shot and killed. This was an earthquake that shook all the believers. There had been so many prophetic words about the long life he would live. How could this be?

The church in Temer-Kala announced three days and nights of fasting and prayer. Many believers were praying for the pastor to be raised from the dead. So-called prophecies and visions rained down with the 'message' that he would be raised. How weary and frustrated I had become with this kind of sensational spirituality! From my experience, and especially at that moment following our forty-day fast, I felt a deep antipathy towards its unhealthy attraction. Everything was always about prophecy, or mystical knowledge, or 'special' revelations, or God's 'special anointed'. It reminded me of my old life, going to fortune tellers, soothsayers and various 'magic' sages. This is a normal thing for people to do when they do not know Christ; they turn to witches and the like in difficult situations. In my culture, people are very 'spiritual', but they often don't discern the origin of the spiritual power. Even religious ministers may not realize the seriousness of witchcraft! I definitely respect the gifts of the Holy Spirit and welcome their full function in healthy Christian life, but it seems that in certain segments of the body of Christ, prophecy and speaking in tongues (see 1 Corinthians 14) are misused or overemphasized.

My husband and I did not feel at peace about participating in that three-day fast. All the same, this tragic event represented a huge sadness for us. Over the years, this pastor was a wise and peaceful brother with a loving, fatherly heart. Despite his continual over-busyness, I always felt significant support and understanding from him. It was beyond belief that he had left us. The identity of his killer remained a mystery. There had been no advance threat or warning.

The unpleasant surprises did not end there. Although we didn't participate in the fast, we stayed in the capital for a period of mourning for our dead pastor. One day while we were with the pastor's family, the phone rang. It was Artur and Aishat, the believers from Dahunsk. People from the mosque had threatened them. In Temer-Kala we immediately asked for widespread prayer on their behalf. A women's conference was scheduled to start in the capital in three days. I was part of the leadership of this conference, which we had been planning since springtime. But Erbulat and I decided that with two days to spare before the conference, we should urgently return to our city and find Artur and Aishat.

Thankfully, we found them right away. They came over to our place, and what a joy to encourage and strengthen them! We had an amazing time together of wonderful fellowship and prayer. The unity was especially precious as we grieved the loss of our beloved pastor and felt the transitory nature of this fragile earthly life. All four of us consecrated our hearts afresh to the Lord. We placed ourselves in his hands and asked him to strengthen us and prepare us for anything that we needed to walk through. Sending them off with prayer, I retired to a far corner of the courtyard to spend time praying alone in preparation for the upcoming conference.

With a peaceful heart, I sat with Bible in hand. As it began to get dark, I turned on a light bulb in the awning above me. No one else was in the courtyard on that summer evening. Suddenly I felt a thick, frightening shadow approach. With every cell of my being I sensed some kind of spiritual evil surrounding me. I began to pray and command the evil power to leave. But the darkness attempted to paralyse me. My legs felt weak. With spiritual eyes, I saw a huge being coming down the stairway from an old room at the back of the house. The being was wrapped in dirty white linen, and its face looked like a dead person. It came towards me. At the same time I sensed many smaller evil beings pushing towards me from all sides. I started calling on the name of Jesus. A desperate spiritual skirmish was underway. I knew that I would not prevail by myself. With all my remaining energy, I dashed to my husband, somewhere inside the house.

At the back door, I screamed with a voice I could hardly recognize, 'Hurry, hurry, help me!'

Erbulat sprinted out, extremely fearful that something horrible had happened to me. Reaching the door, he too sensed the evil. We prayed loudly to the Most High, worshipping him and confessing the truth of the Word of God. It was a real spiritual battle. I can't say how much time went by in prayer and exercising the authority of Jesus. Eventually we sensed that the darkness had dissipated, and a breakthrough of victory had come to our spirits.

With peaceful hearts, we lay down to sleep that night. Nonetheless, I felt that we should be prepared for serious trials ahead. At the same time, I was certain that with God's help, our family would overcome. 'How important it was that we observed that forty-day fast,' I thought. God had prepared us in advance.

But we didn't get even one night's sleep.

Hardly had we lain down when the phone rang. In deep agitation, Artur told us that four vehicles with armed men were coming to their house. They had phoned him and threatened death for 'betrayal of the Muslim faith'. We jumped out of bed and made connections with our network of believers in the capital for urgent prayer. We began praying for the leading of the Holy Spirit and God's protection for us and for our friends. Erbulat called Artur back, but the man who picked up the phone spoke in an aggressive voice.

Everything happened so fast. We understood the strong possibility that unwelcome guests could arrive at our place at any moment. All we could do through the night was pray. When morning came, there was no way of finding out where our friends were or what was happening. Early that morning, our Christian friends from Temer-Kala called and urged us to leave Dahunsk immediately.

But still we didn't hurry. Our friends, our dear brother and sister, were in terrible danger. How could we leave? Were they even alive? For two more hours we prayed for the Holy Spirit's leading. Should we stay and search for them, or drive to Temer-Kala? In prayer we received clear certainty that we needed to leave, and leave promptly. We would go to our church in Temer-Kala where I was to help lead the women's conference. We left that hour.

As soon as the conference was completed, we called our landlady. 'Do you know anything about Artur and Aishat?'

Within minutes of our departure, she told us, a band of armed men had come to the house looking for us. She told them that we had left the city. They attempted to force their way into our rooms and conduct a search, but our landlady, never the timid type, resolutely objected and forbade them to enter. 'I am the owner of this house!' she had insisted.

At this moment we discovered the impact of our witness, which had been conveyed, not through words, but almost entirely by our lives and actions. Our landlady, along with other neighbours, had noisily told these armed men that we were good people and had done nothing but good for all those around us. She urged us not to return. Several armed men kept coming by the house, seemingly checking on us. She had been ordered not to say anything to us. However, she was upset by all this injustice, and decided to warn us anyway.

We shared the news with our brothers and sisters, and asked for prayer support. Almost immediately someone had a 'prophecy' that we were not to return. But, in my heart, I didn't feel a confirmation of that.

Erbulat and I and our two children gave ourselves to a three-day fast, to seek the Lord for his direction. In the face of such difficulties, we didn't want to be controlled by fear. But what was God's will? To return was risky, but danger doesn't always mean stepping back.

At the end of our fast, all four of us were in unity that it was God's will for us to return. Amina, the youngest in the family, said, 'It's possible that only by our returning will some of those men, the ones who are persecuting us, hear the word of Christ.' This word was especially valuable. After prayer with the brothers and sisters, Erbulat and I, with the two children, set off for Dahunsk. We did not know what the future would hold, but we were certain that the Holy Spirit was leading us this way and that God had his plan.

We arrived home late in the evening. The very next morning, armed police came to our house and requested that my husband go with them for questioning. The leader handled himself politely, probably to avoid arousing attention in the neighbourhood. But at this point, not arousing the attention of our good neighbours was *not* going to happen. They were around and slowed things down. Only at this moment did I fully realize why the Lord had led us to this house in the first place. If we had not been sharing a house with our landlady, our enemies would have likely destroyed us right then without any trial or trace.

While Erbulat conversed with the police and inquired of their purposes, I sewed all the pockets closed in his 'going-away clothing'. I knew that a common tactic of hostile authorities was to insert narcotics into the pockets of the accused – and then use it as evidence of the victim's guilt.

While my husband changed into his good clothing, I firmly told the police that I was going with him. 'Wherever he is, I will be there with him! You can line up a whole range of artillery, and I will still not stay home!' The police captain tried to object, but seeing my determination, he became quiet. We got in the vehicle.

'I know where the police station is located. Why are we go-ing in the opposite direction?' I dared to ask, as we headed down the road out of town.

Just beyond the edge of town, the car stopped at an abandoned concrete garage. The scene looked like one of those violent movies. Standing around the building were powerful-looking, heavily armed men. The head of this group scowled and spewed abuse at my husband. One false accusation and degrading word after another came out of his mouth. We could only stand silently. Our 'crime' consisted of preaching Christ. Other things were said with not the slightest connec-tion to reality. They were preparing to beat my husband within an inch of his life. For me, the plan was an assault of the most barbaric nature. They even spoke of doing horrendous things to our children, who had stayed at home.

'Oh, Lord, how can there be so much hate, so much irra-tional, incomprehensible cruelty in these precious men who were created in your image and for your glory? How can one love such crazed and vicious creatures with your unconditional love?' I couldn't see any resemblance to the image of God in their evil and false religious ideology. I thought of the Christian couple who had perished more than a decade before, accused of stealing children to sell their internal organs. What kind of absurdity would these people think up about us?

I had said hundreds of times, 'Lord, I want to follow you, whatever it means. Your will be done, not mine!' It's simple to sing songs about your readiness to follow the Lord to the ends of the earth, sitting in a comfortable church building, when nothing threatens you. But when they are going to cripple your husband before your eyes, attack your children, or assault you, are you ready to faithfully follow him to the end, shining the light of Christ even to your executioner, as Christ did? Only

Christ can give the power to walk the path that he walked. 'Forgive them, Lord, for they don't know what they do!'

'To the prison cells with them!' our inquisitor snarled. As they pushed us into the back seat of the car, I managed to grab a few seconds to connect a phone call to a prayer leader for their urgent prayer support.

The men assigned a police officer to us who was not supposed to ever be a step away from us. Praise to our wonderful Saviour! When the car started, we spoke to him the whole way about the love of Christ. The longer we conversed, the less antagonistic he became. He must have been amazed to discover that we were actually normal, God-fearing people, and not shaking with fear. The more we spoke, the more he listened, with greater and greater interest. Although I knew very well that we might never return home, his interest served as a precious comfort in the midst of the nightmare.

Many thoughts ran through me. 'Lord, I haven't accomplished much of anything for you yet! So many things are unfinished.' There was so much more I wanted to do for the Lord before I stood in his presence.

It was a Sunday morning, and I knew that many fellowships in various countries were meeting and praying for us. Nonetheless, the oppression of evil was strong. It felt like all hell was arrayed against us, and we stood alone.

'Lord, strengthen me! If possible, rescue us, and give us the strength to go through what awaits!' I prayed. 'Lord, I'll go through whatever is necessary, but please, not sexual assault.'

When the police chief arrived, he would interrogate us, we were told. About two hours later, he got there. This was the same man who had viciously screamed at us at the garage. To my amazement he called me into his office alone. When I entered, he addressed me by my first name. He was a former fan of my music. Recognizing who I was, he had decided to speak first with me, one-to-one, before deciding on further steps.

Now I realized the full plan! When they took us to the garage, they intended to eliminate my husband. If I had remained at home, I would never have seen him again on this earth. But when this man recognized me as the former famous singer, he changed the plan of action. Praise to the Most High. He is able to use all things for his good!

Using both persuasion and nasty threats, the police chief tried to get me to turn back to Islam, but his intensity was considerably weaker than at the garage. He claimed that Artur and Aishat had given in and returned to Islam. Of course, I didn't believe him; it was almost certainly a lie. Even if it were partially true, I would never judge them. They had two small children, and Aishat was about to give birth to their third. I could vividly picture the nightmare that these men had subjected them to. Those in positions of power are capable of evoking fear, even terror, in the strongest of people. They are probably not even aware of how they become channels of unrestrained evil. But the one who lives in me has defeated the power of evil. He won that victory with the powerful weapon of unstoppable love. I leaned on his grace and held on to the hope that we could continue to serve him in Dahunsk.

The chief was certain of his rightness. He outlined the horrible torment that awaited us if he released us into the hands of the crowd. He said his men planned to search our place and burn all our belongings. Again, he spoke of vicious plans for our children.

Turmoil swirled within, but I kept a calm and peaceful countenance. 'Don't you fear unpleasant consequences?' I asked. He visibly reacted and stoutly insisted that no, he didn't fear unpleasantness. I don't know how he interpreted my bold question, but it was evident that he was shocked by my peaceful, calm spirit.

Suddenly he changed the tone of his voice. At his own risk and danger, he would give us two hours to permanently leave this city. His policemen would stand by and confirm our departure. This was the only thing he could do for us. If he took his policemen away, we would fall into the hands of the crowd, and then no one and nothing could save us. So the police escorted us home to gather our things and our children, and leave the city promptly.

At home, our children had not been wasting time. After we had been taken away, they had started praying. The idea came to them to gather up all our Christian literature and conceal it. They packed everything into boxes, and wrote on the boxes 'Canned Tomatoes', 'Canned Pickles'. They put the boxes into a storage area in the basement. It never occurred to me that they would think of something like that; they were only thirteen and fifteen years old. Praise to the Lord, who never leaves us or forsakes us!

As for the policeman assigned to us, God had a special plan. We had some amazing interaction with him, right in the midst of these most unusual circumstances. As we organized ourselves, we continued to talk to him about our faith, about who gives us peace, confidence, hope and joy – even in tough times like this.

We were supposed to pack up our whole apartment in two hours. Seeing that we weren't in a panic and weren't even trying to pack everything, the policeman actually started helping us. Our peacefulness amazed him and worked in our favour. You could see the cogs turning in his head; we weren't the kind of people he had expected.

At one point I started pouring out my heart. 'We don't need much in this world. These are only things. We don't need to worry about them, but rather about the souls of people who stay trapped in the darkness, who turn away from their own salvation! If they only understood what they're doing, and who they are rejecting!' My voice was full of grief. With some regret, the policeman said he was just fulfilling his official responsibilities.

Dahunsk and the surrounding region are full of turbulence and criminal activity. There are many terrorist radicals and armed bands. In the policeman's work, he was constantly surrounded by pressure and tension. I felt genuinely bad for him and offered him a New Testament as a gift. At first he recoiled from the Bible, like from fire. I quietly laid the book aside on a table and went into the other room. When I returned, the Bible wasn't there. May God's kind and loving goodwill be fulfilled in the life of this precious man.

The circle of believers in Temer-Kala sent a van. We loaded the van, and – escorted by the police car – drove out of Dahunsk, this city that we loved so much. It was unbearably painful to leave these people – like the pain of having a child taken away. When the police car turned back to the city, Erbulat and I said to our children, 'You can lose everything in this world, even give up your parents – but from Jesus, don't you ever turn away, even if they torture us before your eyes. Remember, any suffering is only temporary, but the Lord lives forever! On this day he delivered us, but at any moment it is possible that you will lose your parents. It's best you be prepared for that, so that you never lose Christ!'

To my husband I said what was burning in my heart ever since that moment we ended up in the hands of those men. 'Don't ever turn away from Jesus, no matter what they do to me, or to our children. Do you promise me?'

'I promise you,' he answered.

'And I promise you,' I said. Driving down the road towards Temer-Kala, all of us seeing clearly what really counted, we gave a full promise to each other and to God to consecrate ourselves to the Lord – to be faithful to him to the end, no matter what the cost. And we prayed that God would strengthen us in this holy consecration.

I truly thank God that he led us through this testing. We were able to look deeply into our hearts. Much was radically changed in our value system, in our understanding of Christian life, and in our service to the Lord. Earlier we had considered ourselves dedicated Christians, but these events were that purifying by fire in the Holy Spirit that the Lord wanted to accomplish in us.

Possessions no longer had any value for us. What would it look like to live the remainder of our days on earth only for his kingdom? There weren't words to adequately express our thankfulness to the Most High for saving us and giving us more time to serve him on the earth.

Something I was very thankful for in those days was discovering that bitterness or rage had not arisen in my heart towards those who had demeaned us. Praise to Christ! There was only love and compassion. This was a huge victory!

But I tell you, love your enemies and pray for those who persecute you, that you may be children of your Father in heaven. He causes his sun to rise on the evil and the good, and sends rain on the righteous and the unrighteous. If you love those who love you, what reward will you get? Are not even the tax collectors doing that? And if you greet only your own people, what are you doing more than others? Do not even pagans do that? Be perfect, therefore, as your heavenly Father is perfect.

Matthew 5:44–48

We urgently wanted to find out where our friends were, and if they were all right. Two days after our expulsion, ignoring the risk, we drove back to the home of Artur's mother in Dahunsk. Although she was a Muslim, we had often conversed with her about Christ, and she related to us with respect and warmth.

When she opened the door and saw us, her face showed shock and fear. It was evident from the pain in her eyes that just seeing us was disturbing. She said that even in a bad dream she would not have wanted to see all that she had lived through in the last few days; but Artur, Aishat and the family were OK. They were under the care of an uncle in another location. We needed to get out of this city as quickly as possible. She didn't want to see any evil happen to us! We were unspeakably thankful that our friends were alive and in a safe place.

If Artur's mother had chosen, one phone call could have doomed us that day, and we never would have departed from that city. We thanked her and blessed her. Before we left, I poured my heart out to her. She had seen with her own eyes the true face of that religion which until now she had defended. She knew our lives, and our love to all. It was for this type of life we were being persecuted.

More than anything in the world we wanted to see Artur and Aishat, but that was impossible. All that we could do was thank the Lord that they were saved, thank him for his mercy and protection – and return to the capital. Truly, God had delivered us from the intentions of the enemy in an amazing way. Not one hair of our heads had fallen to the ground. But it was incredibly painful to leave that region.

'Lord, we never imagined that so suddenly and unexpectedly we would be thrown out of there. You didn't warn us! We didn't know anything. How could that be?' With tears, I vented all this to God, and the Lord immediately replied, 'Everyone wants to know. I want trust. Are you ready to follow me, not holding on to anything, just like a sheep follows her shepherd, not knowing what awaits?' This revelation turned my previous concept of following Christ upside down.

Everyone wants to know. But God wants trust! Knowledge, revelation and prophecy have already been given to us in the Bible. When the Lord gives a word of personal revelation, it is always in agreement with his holy Word. His true words to us are never ripped out of context from his holy Word, or from the purpose and spirit of his Word. But we often look for some mystical 'knowledge' or 'special revelation' given to us with flattering lips. It is not surprising that we fall into many harmful traps. In contrast, it's really very simple. We need to do what is told us in his Word – follow after the Lord with full obedience and trust. If we live in this way, the Holy Spirit will have full access to guide us and transform us continually.

After this breakthrough, my spiritual life became a lot more stable. What a blessing – to simply follow the Lord, fully trusting him and his holy written Word. Such a simple – and such a difficult – path!

14

A Future in God's Love

For a whole year after our return from Dahunsk, my heart was troubled with questions about suffering and the martyrdom of God's holy ones. I struggled to come to peace about this. Yes, God is God, and he has given complete free will to humanity, but will he really allow humans to do absolutely anything? My heart ran cold with the recurring thoughts about the sexual assaults that happen, especially against children. How can God allow such evil? My heart boiled and seethed from outrage about this sin. For a whole year I poured my questions out to the Lord, imagining all sorts of scenarios of torture and agony to test myself, preparing to endure anything. No one knew what was going on inside me. The conversation was only between God and me. In the church, suffering for Christ and paying the highest price is not a popular theme.

A sister from our fellowship came to see me. She brought a book she had had sitting on a shelf. She had a strong feeling that she wanted to give it to me.

When I saw the cover of the book I almost fell over. It was *Hearts of Fire* by The Voice of the Martyrs. In this book were the stories of eight women from various countries of the world, all of them contemporaries of mine. These women had each endured incomprehensible forms of torture due to their faith in Christ.

After reading the book, my questions fell away. Yes, the Lord may allow what he considers necessary, but he will never allow anything beyond what I can bear. He will never leave his servants without support and comfort. Most importantly, whatever trials come into our lives, they are of short duration in comparison to the eternal glory that awaits us in Christ. I came to total trust in my Lord about this question. Indeed, no one and nothing will ever snatch me out of his hands, so long as I remain faithful. As I said earlier to our children, in this sinful world you could lose everything, but never lose your holy God. No matter what the circumstance, don't ever turn away from him!

That entire year, after our sudden departure from Dahunsk, the four of us lived in my apartment in Temer-Kala. We squeezed into one large room with a corner kitchen. But how could I function in this tiny apartment where there was almost no possibility to be alone with my husband for prayer or personal time? My sphere of life had contracted considerably.

'Lord, I want to serve you with all my heart,' I prayed, 'and not just be occupied with small, everyday things. I want to pray, fast, study your Word and preach it.' But what did it mean to follow Christ in *these* conditions? True Christianity is neither holy solitude nor glory on the public stage; it's a daily dying of the ego; sacrificial service in any conditions. The Holy Spirit, my wise Teacher, again opened my eyes and taught me a lesson. Fasting, prayer and the Word of God – these are the keys to life in Christ. They do not require certain external conditions; they are what change your relationship to any condition you find yourself in.

How good the Lord is! Once again he taught me much in these new surroundings. 'Are you ready to serve where no one sees you?' he asked, 'where no one publicly honours you, where maybe no one understands you, except God? Then serve these children with all your heart. Disciple them.'

Suddenly I saw the all-too-common shortfall of church workers too busy with church activities to have any time or energy left for their families. Sunday school is not enough. The world is difficult. And parents are the ones commanded by the Lord to nurture and train their children. Responsibility for the sons and daughters lies on the shoulders of the father and mother.

A minister in a public position feels called and useful. You're a star! But I am a servant of the Lord; what difference does it make where he asks me to serve? Is it less honourable to minister to a helpless old person? Or to a dirty, grumpy, invalid neighbour? Or to children who aren't your biological offspring, to genuinely serve them without fuss or discussion?

In this way, a new chapter in my Christian life began. Under the Holy Spirit's direction, my ministry focus that year became our family. God began to teach me how to be a real servant of Christ at home.

How much easier it is to serve outside the family and be held up as an example of Christian life. In public, it's easier to show only our good qualities. In the security of the home, where we know we're loved, the negative stuff inside pops out. This intensifies when living conditions are more rugged, less comfortable. Now the Holy Spirit was free to work, purging the negative junk by the transforming power of God's love through the cross of Christ.

This is not simple. And it's not automatic. The kingdom of God is righteousness, peace and joy in the Holy Spirit. If this new kingdom is real, it is internal and by the power of the Spirit.

> For the kingdom of God is not a matter of eating and drinking, but of righteousness, peace and joy in the Holy Spirit.
>
> Romans 14:17

Only in God could I come to peace about this being my life. With Manop, we were four in this cramped apartment. Every evening we had a family meeting. We read the Word, prayed and simply interacted with the thoughts and world of our children. We listened and conversed about what was important to them. Praise to God! These regular meetings played a decisive role in establishing our family as a strong, healthy, united team. God's Word was powerful in those times. Rarely was there an evening where there wasn't repentance and forgiveness, especially in the early months. We learned together to admit our mistakes, ask for forgiveness, forgive and reconcile. We learned to be patient, trust, take steps of improvement, and in the end, to simply love each other genuinely, accept each other unconditionally, and find joy together. This was one of the most influential times of growth in my entire life. And it impacted the destinies of two precious young adults, Amina and Manop.

How I rejoiced when both of our children wanted to pray thorough cleansing prayers with us. Thanks to our evening meetings and the work of the Holy Spirit, they experienced precious purifying from the Lord. Many an adult Christian has never come to the point of total honesty and transparency that I saw in Amina and Manop. God worked powerfully in this; all praise and thanks to him!

What a wonderful surprise it was when our son thanked me for becoming mother to him and his sister, and for teaching them to grow strong in God. It scared him to even imagine what their lives would have been like without me. Amina added her words of agreement. Those words were worth far more than any difficulties and pain we might have walked through. God pours out his Holy Spirit into open hearts, and his Spirit transforms us into his image through his all-conquering love.

That year in the tiny apartment was extremely precious and valuable to us. I needed to back away from public Christian leadership until I had learned to serve honestly in humble and real human situations – in my family at home, among my relatives near and distant, my clan circle, those who slandered and insulted me for the name of Christ. I wanted to learn to bring myself as a living and holy sacrifice to the Lord. This is the most excellent way, the way that leads to the most unassailable closeness to the Spirit of the living God.

In that wonderful, difficult year, God took from me the heavy load of public ministry, and freed me to finish the first version of this book. It was birthed in fasting, prayer and tears. I was also able to complete a CD of my songs. I had been using music in my ministry, singing a few songs before and after speaking. Freed to create in new ways since my study in South Africa, I saw people's hearts touched by my singing, even when they didn't understand the language I was singing in. Completing both the book and the CD felt like I had run a long-distance race and finally crossed the finish line! What was next?

'Lord, what do you want to do with me?' I prayed.

In mid-June 2011, I walked out of a Moscow publishing house holding my new book. It was like my little child. Someone had once prophesied that I would hold this book in my hand, but at that time it had seemed totally impossible. Now here it was. My heart overflowed with joy as I inhaled the aroma of the fresh pages and ink.

Clutching my new book, I went to the home of a close friend. I was tired, but satisfied, and soon fell asleep. That night I had a vivid dream. I was in a room, filled with obviously valuable spiritual books on every side. On a table in the room were pens and notebooks. In the centre of the room stood our former pastor, who had been killed the previous year. He was radiant, clothed in a snow-white garment. He praised God and then turned to me. 'If you didn't have to worry about finances or anything else, what would you give yourself to?'

With great enthusiasm, I indicated the room full of books. 'Oh, just to study all this wisdom; I love to explore the Word of God and give the knowledge to others!'

'That's what the Lord is expecting from you!' the pastor exclaimed, shining even brighter.

I woke, greatly encouraged. Could it be that the Lord planned for me to pursue graduate studies?

I returned from Moscow in July, and the four of us decided on a three-day fast to seek the Lord's guidance and clarity as to our next step. We received an answer from him, and all of us had peace in our hearts about it.

With the blessing of our church, we moved to a town two hours outside Moscow. The Lord had gone before us and provided an apartment one block from the best school in the city for our children. He even opened the door for them to the advanced classes. He also provided a job for my husband. The salary was very small, just enough to pay for accommodation. But the Lord continued to provide for us in different amazing ways.

It was also a real step by faith to embark on further study. With Erbulat's support, I enrolled in a respected theological institute. During my first visit to the institute I met the head person. He proposed to support me with some special scholarship money they had. We became very good friends. Sometimes he himself paid for me. He is our senior pastor now.

Never have we found ourselves in financial need. Every new study term felt like a holiday. Each new set of courses gave me the opportunity to interact with intellectual spiritual giants and plunge deeply into the unsearchable riches of God's truth. On top of that, in conjunction with my theological studies, the Institute for Bible Translation in Moscow offered me the opportunity to study the original languages of the Bible. This was in preparation for me to become a theological editor and translator. They secured one of the best specialists in biblical languages as my tutor, and proposed to pay for all my classes. Could I even have dreamed of this?

> Oh, the depth of the riches of the wisdom and knowledge of God!
> How unsearchable his judgments,
> and his paths beyond tracing out!
> 'Who has known the mind of the Lord?
>   Or who has been his counsellor?'
> 'Who has ever given to God,
>   that God should repay them?'
> For from him and through him and for him are all things.
> To him be the glory forever! Amen.
>
> Romans 11:33–36

I struggled with those who assert that the Holy Spirit teaches us everything and we have no need of theological education. At the theological institute, I found many amazingly gifted ministers, pastors and bishops who encouraged me. They served as examples of godliness for me to emulate. Fellowship with a number of these was healing ointment to my spiritual heart. Thanks to them, I was invited many times to preach the Word and share my testimony in churches in the region.

Once in this new place I came under attack from Satan. One night I suddenly awakened. I was immobilized, paralysed, and couldn't even make a sound. Right in front of me I saw a large spiritual being with the appearance of a man wearing a black robe and hood. I had the immediate sense that it was a satanic presence. I couldn't see a face, but I could feel the hate. I struggled to cry out to Jesus, but managed to make only a small, inarticulate sound. With that, my husband awoke. He heard my groans, grabbed me by the shoulders, and shook me free. I called on the name of Jesus – and the apparition suddenly disappeared.

The next day God's Spirit spoke decisively to me: 'Shaadia, remember, the devil is a defeated foe. He only functions through lies, deception and false representations.' This helped me greatly. I didn't need to be knocked around any more by the enemy's paltry, pitiful lies. Jesus has already totally won, and I'm in him. From that day on I took a new place of victory in my position in Christ.

> Submit yourselves, then, to God. Resist the devil, and he will flee from you . . . Humble yourselves before the Lord, and he will lift you up.
>
> James 4:7,10

> And God raised us up with Christ and seated us with him in the heavenly realms in Christ Jesus, in order that in the coming ages he might show the incomparable riches of his grace, expressed in his kindness to us in Christ Jesus.
>
> Ephesians 2:6,7

One major victory was yet ahead – regarding my personal calling in the Lord. I still had questions. Maybe it had only seemed that God had called me to study the Word and preach? Perhaps all the prophecies about my life were mistaken? What was I to do with the widely held outlook in many church circles that women were not allowed to preach or teach? They should only remain silent in church, busy themselves with household duties, and so on. With all my strength, I honestly tried to live that way – but my husband was of a different opinion. This became the next human-made stereotype which I needed to be set free from. We must read the Bible in the context of the times!

I thank God for my husband, who was himself free from any narrow traditional biases. Before our wedding, my future husband expressed to me that he knew God had sent him into my life to be a rock, a tower of strength, to enable me to fulfil the calling God had placed on my life. My beloved life partner had continued to be firm in his conviction and neither men in the church, nor I myself, had moved him one iota from his certainty on this. Subsequently I was the one who needed to change and get free from false teachings and oppressive human traditions. The strength of my husband was a huge factor in enabling me to fulfil the calling of the Eternal One in my life.

However, it took some time and there was a considerable struggle before I eventually felt a sense of peace and began to function freely in my callings. Definitive closure on this matter came about only after a tough trial I experienced. Having moved from a warm climate to a considerably colder northern climate, I wasn't immediately prepared for the adjustments. One day we attended an outdoor event, organized by our friends, and too late I realized I was not dressed warmly enough. During the two or three hours outside, I nearly froze. After returning home, I came down with a suffocating cough. This congestion worsened day by day. I developed a severe sore throat, so bad that I could hardly swallow, and my body temperature dropped dangerously 3 degrees below normal. This developed into cystitis and every bone and muscle in my body ached – followed by splitting headaches. I tried every conceivable medicine. And we cried out to the Lord in prayer! But my condition only worsened.

This battle went on for almost six weeks. One day, struggling into the kitchen to make a hot drink for myself, I clearly heard these words inside my heart: 'The devil has arisen against you and your ministry calling. It's crucial that you go to fasting with prayer.' This divine voice was decisive and strong. Right then an inner strength stirred within me, along with steely resolve – 'Enough is enough! All right! I'm not going to put up with this any longer. The enemy will lose this one!' I articulated all of this out loud in the name of the Lord, and resolved to start a fast immediately.

Granted, from a human point of view, fasting at this point was either impossible or unwise. I was dealing with a severe inflammation of the respiratory system, extreme pain, abnormally low temperature and near-total exhaustion. The constant cough tormented me so much that I could hardly sleep, breathe, or even talk. But I had absolutely no doubt that this was a spiritual battle and only spiritual weapons would win it. When I began, I anticipated the fast would be longer – but in reality I only fasted five days from food, taking just water to drink.

This was a severe battle. I experienced such terrible pain throughout my body – the bones and muscles – that only strong faith, spiritual determination and focus on victory in the name of Christ were what gave me strength to prevail. The pain was so great that even the voices of my beloved family or their presence with me in a room seemed to intensify my suffering. I had to ask everyone to 'please leave me alone and don't come into my room'. I mostly just tossed and turned in my bed, constantly calling out to the Lord and praising his name. When the spasms of pain intensified, I would moan, 'Lord, have mercy on me!'

On the third day of the fast, the cough which had plagued me for six weeks began to disappear. What joy it was to start breathing normally! On the fourth day, by evening, I gradually began to realize that I was healed. The darkness lifted, although a few symptoms still lingered. The Lord showed me in a vision that a tightly woven, dark, oppressive cloud over me had suddenly shattered into a million pieces. Clear blue sky opened above my head, full of radiant light.

During that night of sleep, before the fifth day, I woke from the sound of the Lord's voice, saying, 'Shaadia, you must preach and teach every month.' From that moment on, every bit of doubt and confusion regarding my holy calling decisively fell away. On the evening of the fifth day I understood that my fast was completed. I still felt some pain remaining in my body. But the Holy Spirit spoke to my heart, 'Who do you believe, your feelings, or the Lord, who has already healed you?' At that second, when I received that, the pain completely left my body. The cough was totally gone and never returned. It was a miracle. For a month and a half I had suffered, and no medicine – even the best I could find – did me any good. But God had a holy plan. He wanted to impart to me one of his most important truths for my life. It required only five days of fasting and prayer in submission to God. By the work of the Holy Spirit, the illness and any trace of it was completely gone. But that in itself wasn't all that important. What was really important was the Lord's word about my calling, which came to me during this trial.

At our church's first Sunday service following this fast, I was asked to preach. Although in earlier years I had served in preaching and teaching, now everything was different. I could feel with my whole being and mind that a huge change had taken place. The hand of God was upon me. Joy, conviction, inner fire – all of which previously came and went incon-sistently – I could now feel vividly and naturally within me. I entered into the place appointed for me by the Lord! The old teachings which severely limited the role of women in the body of Christ had prevented me from spreading my wings and moving freely in the divine calling, and now they lost all power over me. I had experienced heavy opposition from some men, trying to discourage me. But the Word of God in many places was much wider on this point than a rigid, narrow rendering. God himself had called me and placed me into this ministry, and the negative no longer touched me. Who can tell him how he is to act? I was ready to fulfil his will with joy!

Now I was released into the Word of God pouring through me, along with studying the biblical languages and my Bible translation work – just as in the vision from years before of the translucent, radiant Bible. And what about my own people? Relational doors are more open to me in my native language group these days, compared to the first years of my conversion. Although threats come time after time, during the last five years (2013–2017) my relationships with some of my relatives and previous friends have improved. As a family, we have used every opportunity to overcome any hatred, to manifest God's love and generosity towards those very precious people right in the midst of the darkest. It is so wonderful to experience how love overcomes, even in the most dreadful situations; to witness how the crucified, humble, serving, respectful love gradually melts hearts. It requires a lot of effort and sacrificial service, but it works powerfully. With all my heart I desire that my own people would come to know the Lord Jesus Christ and be filled with his love. I dream about this more than anything in the world. If I could only live to see this with my own eyes, there is nothing else I long for on this earth. And even if I don't see it with my own eyes, I will continue to pray for this until I have drawn my last breath, and I will offer the hope of Jesus to my people with every fibre of my being as long as I live on this earth.

For every person, the Lord has prepared their unique path. I am walking on his path for me, but I have only just begun and have only come to know him a little. Today the hunger in my heart for his fullness is more than it ever was before. I am hungry and thirsty for him, but I can already testify and thank him for all his generosity which he has abundantly poured into my life. When I look at myself from the perspective of a typical human being, I am amazed at his miraculous working in my life. The wisest thing I ever did was give my heart and my life – my internal being and my external behaviour – to my Saviour.

> Why, you do not even know what will happen tomorrow. What is your life? You are a mist that appears for a little while and then vanishes.
>
> James 4:14

Not long ago, I attended the funeral of one of my closest female relatives. She was a Muslim. At one time, due to my conversion to Christ, she had been furious with me. But when she was seriously ill, the relationship softened, and I was able to speak with her about spiritual things. She left this life at a tragically young age for an unknown eternal destination. It seemed to me as if it was only yesterday that we walked to school together, without the slightest thought of the shortness of human life. She was a good-hearted person, full of the joy of life and generous to all – and she so much wanted to live!

During the time that she was ill, I prayed fervently for her healing and asked God for a miracle. The Lord always answers our prayers, but sometimes he does not answer in the way that we would like. And so, sitting at her funeral, I comforted myself with the hope that the things I had told her before her death had not been in vain, and we might yet be together in the eternal kingdom of our Creator and heavenly Father.

Symptoms of the illness that killed her had been apparent much earlier. For a long time, she hoped that somehow it would all go away. She applied pain-killing salves to the affected area and kept on working. But the time came when it was no longer possible to hide her condition. The anesthetizing salves no longer helped; she had to seek new treatments; but it was too late. No longer could she deny the reality to herself or to anyone else, and she came face-to-face with this terrible illness called 'cancer'.

My relative's story illustrates the spiritual condition of every human being. We are all stricken by a fatal illness called 'sin' – an illness ultimately far more horrible than cancer. This illness causes great suffering. The devil proposes to each person various types of 'anesthetizing salves': career, education, money, pleasure, physical beauty, 'religion', fame, cultural identity, human tradition, even service in the name of God. Not thinking about the horrible consequences of their choice, the person often satiates him or herself with the outward and short-term 'antidote'. Many people are smart enough to continue in this manner for a long time – to the eyes of the world, often with considerable success – although all the while inside they are experiencing serious pain.

But inevitably, in the life of every person, that moment arrives when those 'anesthetizing meds' are not enough. All the masks are gone, and they stand before the Creator absolutely naked, face-to-face with that horrible, destructive illness by the name of 'sin', which has infected them from the very beginning of life. At that moment, the real consequences of a long-term denial will be inescapable for every person.

Throughout their lives, human beings can choose to hide in a crowd, but when it comes to facing God, death and eternity, every human being will come completely alone. If a person has not dealt honestly with the illness of 'sin' in life, it is too late at that point. No one wants eternal death in the gloomy darkness of hell; everyone hopes for eternal life.

If you identify with my search for life, then run to Jesus, the sole Source of life, hope and love – and you will find forgiveness of your sins and life everlasting.

For those who already know Christ, I pray that you will treasure what you have been given. Walk fully with the Most High God, the Eternal One. Consecrate your heart and your life totally to him. Do not put off necessary cleansing, because time is fleeting and 'the days are evil' (Ephesians 5:16). Living in Christ is so simple and yet so difficult, but his love triumphs over everything!

Dear friends, let us love one another, for love comes from God. Everyone who loves has been born of God and knows God. Whoever does not love does not know God, because God is love. This is how God showed his love among us: he sent his one and only Son into the world that we might live through him.

1 John 4:7–9

Conclusion

Dear reader, perhaps it was hard for you to read this book to the end: 'too much pain and suffering' as some people have told me in their reviews in the Russian version, even though it gives only a general description of my life.

But I think my story is, to some extent, similar to many others. Each of us is deprived of the glory of God and alienated from God. This book is written solely thanks to the work of the Holy Spirit in my life. Now, looking back, I just marvel at how wonderful, great and perfect are the works of God. He has all the dates and timing in his hands. Nothing is accidental.

The Russian version of this book was written, in parallel with my other duties, from 2008 until it was published in June, 2011. Delving into this story again, in the process of its translation into English and subsequent editing, I suddenly realized that I could never write such a book again. Perhaps I'll write another book, but it will be different. There is another season in my life now. This book reflects a special time when the Lord drew me to himself, pulled me out of sin and death, and transformed me from a broken and filthy vessel into a vessel of his glory. Yes, I had to endure a lot of things, and I made a lot of mistakes, until I met the Lord. And then in the Lord I had to go through a lot of agony and anxiety in the process of my healing. But I wanted, and want, the Lord to make all that he pleases of my life. I am convinced that the Lord will go so far and deep in your life depending on how much you agree to allow him.

The main point I want to emphasize at the end of my book is this: that the Lord was merciful to me and offered me his hand – and I, in turn, tightly took hold of this hand. This is the great miracle, when his invisible hand makes visible miracles of transformation in the lives of real people. Owing to this, I am his living testimony today. Everything that had previously caused me great pain and anguish has become an amazing story, a history which can bring hope and freedom to the lives of many other people. How did this happen? Why did I respond to his call? And why do many others not hear his call?

The more I serve the Lord and follow him, the more I realize that I have no answer to this question. This is a great mystery to me. But everything that has happened to me, it was only by the grace of God. Only in this can I be sure: his amazing incomprehensible love and mercy. What can I give him in return? Nothing! Myself? Did I belong to myself? That I live, breathe, move and have my being is only to his credit.

When I think about the Lord, about God's plan, about humanity's destiny, my heart is filled with boundless joy, gratitude and reverence. What great love is manifested to us on this earth, and each of us is given a free choice. The choice is perhaps all we have – the free will of choice. My free-will choice is aimed only at one thing: it's a burning desire every day to live only for him, in him and by him, glorifying his name in everything in my life, always remembering the limitations of my earthly existence and the brevity of the earthly journey.

We need to use our time to do all that is possible on this earth so that at the end we will stand before him and hear:

Good and faithful servant . . . Enter into the joy of your Lord.

Matthew 25:21, NKJV

This is worth living for! Today I work for the Lord full-time, and there is nothing else I want in life.

According to the doctors I was supposed to be in a wheelchair today – fully paralysed and unable to speak, see, hear and even to think. Five years ago, in July 2012, I was ordered to be under strict medical supervision for the rest of my life, and to go to the hospital half-yearly in order to undergo treatment; every six months I was to have an MRI of my entire spine. I was not to have any burden, mental or physical. They guaranteed me a dramatic deterioration of my health, and the need to do a complex operation on my spine. But, after prayer and passionate pursuit of God's face, my husband and I refused all this. I don't want to live such a life! Instead, I stood under the constant supervision of my Great Only Perfect Doctor and began to work in his fields with even greater zeal. Today I carry tremendous loads, both mentally and physically. I know what pain is. Not just once have I cried before the Lord and prayed, for he is able to free us from all infirmities and diseases.

How easy it would be to work and how much we could get done if we were pain-free. But I have realized one thing. To follow the Lord and serve him wholeheartedly, we don't need comfortable conditions but faith, trust and obedience to God. And the rest he will add because he has promised it. His grace is enough for each day. And I testify that his grace is more than enough for me personally each day. My life is not dependent on the condition of the spine or other parts of my body, but only on the One who gives me the breath of life. He's the last word. How sweet and exciting to trust the Lord and to be in his hand!

Glory to the Lord for everything and forever!

Appendix:

Prayer

I offer here the example of a simple prayer, as a help to any who would like to receive the gift of grace through Jesus Christ, the atoning sacrifice for your sins. This is for those who are ready to turn away from all false gods and idols in their lives and open their lives fully to the true Creator. This Creator God is the one who sent Jesus Christ into the world as an atoning sacrifice for the sins of all humanity. Let these words be your own sincere prayer, issuing from your own soul.

My dear heavenly Father,
I confess that I am a sinner and ask for your forgiveness for all my sins. Thank you that you gave your only Son as an atoning sacrifice for my sins. Have mercy on me, forgive me, cleanse me, sanctify me and fill me with your presence through the grace of this wonderful sacrifice.

Jesus, thank you that you took upon yourself all my guilt and punishment. Come into my life and reign in me totally. I ask you to wash me, cleanse me and change my life from the inside out, according to your holy will for my life. I now repudiate sin and death and welcome your grace and fullness of life in the power of your Spirit.

Thank you, my heavenly Father, that you waited for me patiently all these years and that you have forgiven me for everything. Help me to walk on this path and into the fullness of life that you have planned for me.

In the name of Jesus Christ, I pray to you.

Amen.

If you have prayed this prayer, with all my heart I congratulate you! I urge you to become part of a local church or fellowship of born-again followers of Jesus Christ, as soon as possible (see John 3:3–7). It is God's plan for you to join his family, where you will find spiritual strength to be established in your knowledge of God and his will. Start reading the Bible, which is God's Word, and let your fellowship with your heavenly Father and his limitless love for you fill your heart with gladness. May our marvellous Lord preserve and strengthen you. I pray that his will be fulfilled in your life and that you not lose out on any of the rewards he has prepared for those who love him.

As it is written:
'What no eye has seen,
    what no ear has heard,
and what no human mind has conceived' –
    the things God has prepared for those who love him.

1 Corinthians 2:9

Bibliography

The following book is referred to in the text.

The Voice of the Martyrs, *Hearts of Fire: Eight Women in the Underground Church and Their Stories of Costly Faith* (Nashville, TN: Thomas Nelson Publishing, 2012).

Notes

1 Pronounced: shah-dee-uh

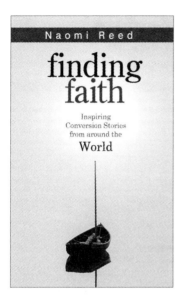

Finding Faith

Inspiring Conversion Stories from around the World

Naomi Reed

'We will have no more Voodoo in our house. It's true that the Voodoo has power, but the One I believe in has much more power. And because of his power, the Voodoo can't hurt you, or any of us, anymore' (Alberic, Benin).

A collection of inspirational stories from around the world, sharing the exciting and life-changing transformation that Jesus brings. From the flat, dry towns of Uganda to northern Iraq, from the land of the native Australians to the former Soviet Union, Naomi Reed shares moving accounts of ordinary people who have put their faith in the Lord Jesus Christ. They all say the same thing . . . God's love is amazing, and it changes everything.

978-1-78078-462-5

'An amazing testament to God's transforming power and the fruitfulness of a surrendered life.' – Chris Bowater

GOD KNOWS WHAT I'M DOING HERE

The incredible story of a mission worker saved from a rebellious past

SHEILA V. LEECH

God Knows What I'm Doing Here

The incredible story of a mission worker saved from a rebellious past

Sheila Leech

Sheila Leech's Sunday school teacher would plead with God, 'Please don't let Sheila come to class today!' As a teenager, she was far from God and taking drugs – until Jesus broke into her life and called her into his service.

For nine years she lived with an indigenous tribe in the Ecuadorian rainforest as a missionary. Having trained as a nurse, she now travels the world serving those affected by war and natural disasters.

A gripping account of her sometimes perilous adventures, Sheila's story demonstrates God's grace and protection, his power and provision, and that he can use anyone who trusts in him, whatever their start in life.

978-1-78078-452-6

God Conversations

Stories of how God speaks and what happens when we listen

Tania Harris

Stories of God talking to his people abound throughout the Bible, but we usually only get the highlights. We read: 'God said "Go to Egypt,"' and then, 'Mary and Joseph left for Egypt.' We're not told how God spoke, how they knew it was him, or how they decided to act on what they'd heard.

In *God Conversations*, international speaker and pastor Tania Harris shares insights from her own story of learning to hear God's voice. You'll get to eavesdrop on some contemporary conversations with God in the light of his communication with the ancients. Part memoir, part teaching, this unique and creative collection will help you to recognize God's voice when he speaks and what happens when you do.

978-1-78078-188-4

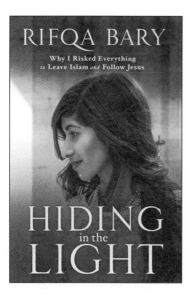

Hiding in the Light

Why I Risked Everything to Leave Islam and Follow Jesus

Rifqa Bary

In 2009, sixteen-year-old Rifqa Bary made national news in the United States when she ran away from her Ohio home, claiming that her father, an observant Muslim, had abused and threatened to kill her because of her Christian faith. The media storm pitted critics of Islam against its defenders, sparking national debate about the treatment of women and converts within Islam and how they should be protected.

In *Hiding in the Light*, Rifqa Bary recounts in riveting detail the events leading up to her decision to leave home and the chain of events that followed. Her story challenges us to consider what it means to sacrifice for faith and to ask ourselves how far we would go to live out what we believe.

978-1-86024-969-3